THE
PRACTICE
OF THE PRESENCE
OF GOD

THE
PRACTICE
OF THE PRESENCE
OF GOD

BROTHER LAWRENCE

Bridge-Logos
Alachua, Florida 32615 USA

Bridge-Logos

Alachua, FL 32615 USA

The Practice of the Presence of God
by Brother Lawrence

Edited by Harold J. Chadwick

Library of Congress Catalog Card Number: 99-69627
International Standard Book Number 978-0-88270-793-8

Unless otherwise indicated, the Scripture quotations in this publication are from the *King James Version* of the Bible. Copyright ©1979, 1980, 1982 Thomas Nelson Inc., Publishers. Used by permission.

Historic information, engravings and photograph are from the original French Edition by Conrad de Meester, *Ecrits et Entrentiens sur la Pratique de la Presence de Dieu*, copyright 1991. Used by permission of Les Editons du Cerf. English Translation copyright by the Washington Province of Discalced Carmelites, Inc., 1994.

Cover art: The Fontenay Abbey, Burgundy, France. From an original photo by Henri Gaud.

G1.319.BM.m901.35250

Contents

Part V Ways of Attaining the Presence of God

Brother Lawrence

(Nicholas Herman c.1605-1691)

That there are no comprehensive biographies of Brother Lawrence is both ironic and perfect—*ironic* because he stands today as a man of profound influence in classic Christian literature and we have a natural curiosity about him, and *perfect* because his life was never about him. He was a simple man who simply served God. In fact, he never even wrote a book. The book you're about to read is a compilation of letters and recollections of conversations that were assembled after his death.

Brother Lawrence was a Carmelite monk who was born Nicholas Herman in the Lorraine province of France sometime around 1605. The date of his birth is inexact because he was born into humble circumstances, and probably no one thought to chronicle the arrival of a child who would influence Christian thinking for centuries to come. He had no education ... and no hope of one.

He was converted to Catholicism in 1629. After serving as a soldier and a footman for some time, he entered into the religious community of the Carmelites in Paris in about 1649. The Carmelite Order of Brother Lawrence's day dates back to 1562 when Teresa of Avila took it upon herself to reform the ancient order of Carmelites (founded in 1190 on Mount Carmel in Israel). It had seriously eroded in an increasingly undisciplined environment. The monks and nuns had begun to take liberties with the basic principles of cloistered life. Teresa resolved to rescue the traditions of the Carmelite nuns by reinstating rules based on truly godly conduct and emphasizing a contemplative life in poverty and service to God. John of the Cross joined Teresa and reformed the practices of the Carmelite monks. The Carmelites—both nuns and monks—were once again a strict order.

It was there, as a lay Carmelite brother, that Nicholas Herman took the name Brother Lawrence. He was assigned to kitchen duty: preparing food and washing dishes and mopping floors. Amidst the steaming pots and pans, he entered into conversation with God. His admitted distaste for kitchen drudgery day in and day out reveals a very human side of Brother Lawrence. But more important, it unlocks the secret of his grace. That he disliked it is beside the point. That he used it to serve God is his gift. He transformed drudgery into devotion, and therein is the lesson we learn as we browse his letters and eavesdrop on conversations held hundreds of years ago.

"The time of business does not differ from the time of prayer, and in the noise and clatter of my kitchen, while several persons are at the same time calling for different things, I possess God in as great tranquility as if I were on my knees at the Blessed Sacrament."

Brother Lawrence says of his constant conversation with God, "I make it my business to rest in His holy presence, which I keep myself in by a habitual, silent, and secret conversation with God. This often causes in me joys and raptures inwardly, and sometimes so outwardly, so great that I am forced to use means to moderate them, and prevent their appearance to others."

It is tempting to think that Brother Lawrence's grace came easily, that he was a serene and joyful monk who smiled and moved gently through his days, but such was not the case. He was, in fact, a very human man prone to anxiety and melancholy. His nature, however, was secondary to his relationship with God. Later in his life, he suffered from sciatic gout, the agony of which forced him from standing in his kitchen. He didn't take to bed, however. He turned to an equally menial, humble task: crafting and repairing sandals for his brothers. But his discipline and strict focus on his continuous communion with God allowed him to overcome every obstacle, even unto death.

During his lifetime, his reputation spread as a man of unusual serenity and devotion to God. His simple message had a profound effect on those who knew of him, and those who knew him personally and sought his counsel. He was even visited by the Pope. He said, "We ought not to grow tired of doing little things for the love of God, who regards not the greatness of the work, but the love with which it is performed." *dad clean my motives and change them to love.*

Brother Lawrence didn't see himself as much of a writer. In a short piece he penned personally, entitled "Life," he noted, "I committed my thoughts some sixty-five times to writing, but comparing what I had written with that which I had just experienced in my soul, I consider it so inferior and so far removed from the inspired thought with which I had just been visited, of the greatness and goodness of God, that often I felt compelled to tear it up at once."

Most of Brother Lawrence's work that we have today consists of conversations and letters that were edited after his death by Abbé de Beaufort and printed in two volumes: *Maximes Spirituelles* in 1692 and *Moeurs et Entretiens du*

3

Frère Laurent in 1694. In the preface of Abbé de Beaufort's edition, we read "[He was] a holy man who all his life had studied to avoid the gaze of men and whose saintliness is only fully seen now that he is dead. Those in the thick of the great world will learn from these Letters how greatly they deceive themselves seeking for peace and joy in the glitter of things that are seen yet temporal. Those who are seeking the Highest Good will gain from this book strength to persevere in the practice of virtue." *What are the virtues.*

About This Book

The "Letters" were written to specific people to deal with particular spiritual problems. One can almost hear Brother Lawrence counseling. And also interesting, the letters afford a privileged glimpse into the intimate lives of men and women who lived in Brother Lawrence's time—surprisingly similar to today.

The "Maxims" are not so personal. They are carefully arranged and reflect mature thinking, indicating that Brother Lawrence might have been attempting to organize his teachings later in his life.

"The Character of Brother Lawrence" is a reflection of his life as others saw him. It is authored by M. Beaufort, who compiled the "Letters and Conversations." In this piece, Beaufort lets Brother Lawrence speak for himself. He writes, "No one can paint the saints as well as they can themselves, and nothing can bring this servant of God more clearly before you than his own words spoken in all the simplicity of his heart."

"Collected Thoughts of Brother Lawrence" was taken from a brief piece he wrote himself in 1691. There are not many thoughts in the collection, and they are somewhat fragmented, but they are worth inclusion.

" ... *his sense of inner peace was so profound that other individuals were drawn to him for spiritual direction.*"

Write.
Worship
Wait on you
Will to love
Water of Word
Welcome others

A surviving portion of Broher Lawrence's monastery in Paris. The structure is now part of the Institut Catholique (photographer unknown). Used by permission.

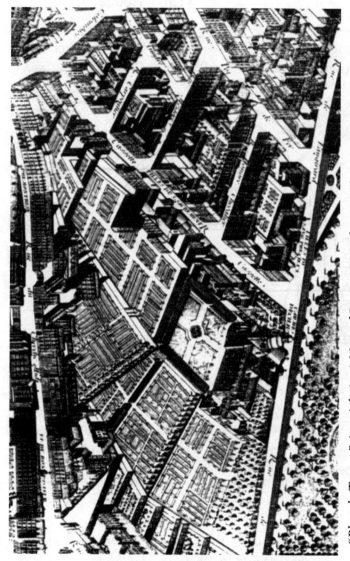

"Plan de Turgot" (partial view) Map of Paris, 1705, showing the monastery and gardens of the Discalced Carmelite Friars. (Courtesy of Father Daniel Ferrand, OCD, Paris, France)

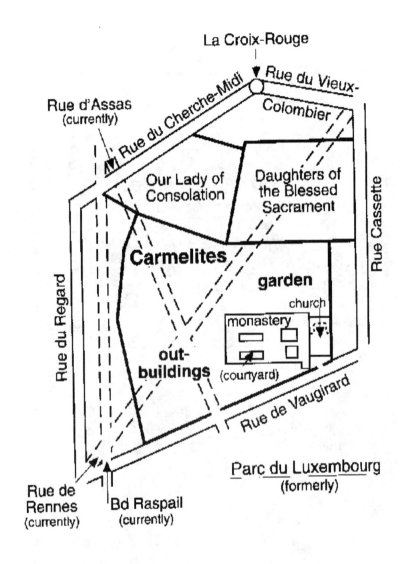

Discalced Carmelite monastery in Paris. Plan of the grounds at the time Brother Lawrence lived there.

The Church of the Discalced Carmelite Friars in Paris as Brother Lawrence knew it. The monastery to the left was considerably enlarged during Brother Lawrence's lifetime. (17th Century engraving by Jean Marot.) Used be permission of the Bibliotheque Nationale de Paris.

The Church of the Discalaced Carmelite Friars in Paris.
(17th Century engraving, author unknown.)
Used by permission of the Bibliotheque Nationale de Paris.

I
Collected Thoughts

Collecteb Thoughts

It matters not to me what I do, or what I suffer, so long as I abide lovingly united to God's will—that is my whole business.

I am in the hands of God, and He has His own good purposes regarding me. I do not concern myself, therefore, about anything that people can do to me. If I cannot serve God here, I will find some place else in which to serve Him.

The practice of the presence of God is the shortest and easiest way to attain to Christian perfection. It is the form and life of virtue. It is the great preservative from sin.

The practice will become easy, if we have but courage and a good will.

The whole world seems to me to be no longer real—all that my outward eyes behold pass like fantasies and dreams.

That which I see with the eyes of the soul is what alone I long for, and to be not yet in the possession of my heart's desire brings me sorrow and drooping of spirit.

On the one hand, I am dazzled by the brightness of the Sun of Righteousness, the Scatterer of the shades of night; while on the other, with my eyes dimmed by my own sin, I feel at times as if I were beside myself.

✱ Yet, I make it my ordinary business to abide in the presence of God with the humility of a useless, though faithful, servant.

Since I first entered the religious life, I have looked on God as the goal and end of all the thoughts and affections of the soul.

As a novice, during the hours appointed for prayer I labored to arrive at a conviction of the truth of the Divine Being, rather by the light of faith than by the deductions of the intellect.

By this short and certain method I grew in the knowledge of this object of love, in whose presence I resolved always to abide.

Possessed thus entirely with the greatness and the majesty of this infinite Being, I went straightway to the place that duty had marked out for me—the kitchen.

There, when I had carried out all that called for me, I gave to prayer whatever time remained, and also prayed before my work and after.

Before beginning any task I would say to God, with childlike trust:

O God, since Thou art with me, and it is Thy will that I must now apply myself to these outward duties, I beseech Thee, assist me with Thy grace that I may continue in Thy presence. To this end, O Lord, be with me in this my work, accept the labor of my hands, and dwell within my heart with all Thy fullness.

Moreover, as I worked, I would continue to hold familiar conversation, offering to Him my little acts of service, and entreating the unfailing assistance of His grace.

When I had finished, I would examine how I had performed my duty. If well, I gave Him thanks. If ill, I besought His pardon.

Then, without losing heart, I set my spirit right, and returned anew to His presence, as though I had never wandered from Him.

Thus, by rising after every fall, and by doing all in faith and love without wearying, I have come to a state in which it would be as little possible for me not to think of God as it was hard to discipline myself to it at the beginning.

O Lord, O God of gods, how wonderful Thou art in all Thy thoughts, beyond our understanding. How profound in all Thy purposes, Almighty in the works of Thy Hands!

All that I have heard people say concerning God, that I have read myself, or perceived of Him in my mind, cannot satisfy me.

Infinite in His perfection, how can He be portrayed, or how can people find words to picture Him?

Faith alone can reveal Him or teach me what He is. By faith I learn more of God, and in a very little time, than I could do in the schools after many a long year.

Oh! Faith, faith; oh! marvelous virtue, which illumines the spirit of people and leads them on to the knowledge of their Creator.

Oh! virtue altogether lovely, so little known, and still less practiced, yet which, once known, is so glorious, so full of unspeakable blessing.

The greatest glory we can give to God is to distrust our own strength utterly, and to commit ourselves wholly to His safekeeping.

O Lord, the sense of Thy love nearly overwhelms me. If it be Thy will, bestow these many tokens of Thy loving-kindness on those who know Thee not, to draw them to Thy service. For me it is enough to have the riches that faith brings in the knowledge of Thee.

Yet, forasmuch as I must not reject the favors of Thy bounteous hand, accept my praises, Lord.

And, I entreat, receive again these gifts, which Thou hast granted; for, Lord, Thou knowest that it is not Thy gifts I seek, but Thee Thyself, and my heart will know no rest, till it has found Thee.

O Lord, enlarge the chambers of my heart that I may find room for Thy love. Sustain me by Thy power, lest the fire of Thy love consume me.

The practice of the presence of God is of very great service in helping us to pray in truth.

It restrains the mind from wandering throughout the day and holds it fixed steadfastly on God.

Thus the mind will more easily remain tranquil in the hour of prayer.

Life is full of perils and of hidden reefs, on which we will shipwreck without the continual assistance of the grace of God. Yet how can we ask for it unless we are with Him?

How can we be with Him unless our thoughts are ever of Him? How can He be in our thoughts unless we form a holy habit of abiding in His presence, there asking for the grace we need each moment of our life?

If you would go forward in the spiritual life, you must avoid relying on the subtle conclusions and fine reasonings of the unaided intellect. Unhappy they who seek to satisfy their desire therein!

✱ The Creator is the great teacher of truth.

We can reason laboriously for many years, but far fuller and deeper is the knowledge of the hidden things of faith and of Himself, which He flashes as light into the heart of the humble.

✱ Nothing can give us so great relief in the trials and sorrows of life as a loving relationship with God.

When such is faithfully practiced, the evils that assail the body will prove light to us.

God often ordains that we should suffer in the body to purify the soul, and to constrain us to abide with Him. How can anyone whose life is hid with God, and whose only desire is God, be capable of feeling pain?

Let us then worship Him in our infirmities, offering to Him our sorrows when they press upon us, and asking Him lovingly as children their dear father to give us strength and mold our will to His.

Brief prayers as these are very proper for all sick persons, and prove a wonderful charm against sorrow.

Ah, if I know that my heart did not love God, I would pluck it out this very instant.

O Loving-Kindness so old and still so new, I was too long before loving Thee.

If you are young, my brother or sister, profit I beseech you from my confession, that I cared too little to employ my early years for God.

Consecrate all yours to His love.

If I had only known Him sooner, if I had only had some one to tell me then what I am telling you, I would not have delayed so long in loving Him.

★ Believe me, count as lost each day you have not used in loving God.

II
Character of
Brother Lawrence

Beginning of Perfection

I am writing down what I have heard and seen myself of the character of Brother Lawrence,[1] who died about two years ago in the <u>Carmelite Monastery at Paris</u>,[2] and whose memory is a sweet savor.

A person who has <u>chosen to be a doorkeeper in the house of God</u>[3] rather than hold a high rank among sinners, who has <u>taken upon him the yoke of Jesus Christ</u>,[4] and preferred it to the empty pomp and pleasures of the world, has asked me to write down for those souls who have been <u>freed from the chain of things seen</u>, what he knew I had collected of the thoughts and precepts of Brother Lawrence.

I obey willingly, and although a sketch of the "Life" and a collection of the "Letters"[5] of this good brother have been already published, it seems to me that we cannot make known too widely <u>what we have preserved of this holy man</u>.

It is my firm belief that I can do no greater service than hold up this man as <u>a pattern of solid piety</u> in an age when almost everyone puts virtue where it is not, and takes false ways to arrive at it.

It will be Brother Lawrence himself who will speak in these pages. In the "Conversations" that I had with him, and which follow this section, <u>I will give you his own words</u>, just as I wrote them down immediately upon leaving him.

No one can paint the saints as well they themselves. The *Confessions* of St. Augustine give us a far more living portrait than anything that others could have added. So nothing can bring more clearly before you this servant of God than his own words spoken in all the simplicity of his heart.

With all his virtue, Brother Lawrence was intensely human. He had a frank open manner, which, when you met him, won your confidence at once, and made you feel that you had found a friend in whom you could confide completely.

On his part, as soon as he knew with whom he was dealing, he spoke quite freely and gave immediate proof of his great goodness of heart. What he said was very simple, but to the point and full of sense.

Beneath a rather rough exterior, one found remarkable wisdom, a spaciousness of mind quite beyond the range of the ordinary poor lay brother, and insight that surpassed all expectation.

As a man of affairs he was capable of carrying through the greatest matters, and of giving wise and safe counsel. Such were the characteristics that struck the ordinary observer.

The disposition of his heart and the inner life of his soul, he has himself depicted in the "Conversations."

His conversion sprung from a high notion that he conceived of the power and wisdom of God,[6] whom ever afterwards he sought diligently and with great faithfulness, driving away all other thoughts.

As this first realization of God was the beginning of the perfection of Brother Lawrence, as it proved to be, it is important that we stop here for a little to consider his conduct at this time.

Faith was the one light he took for his path, and not only did it afford him his first glimpse of God, but he never desired any other lamp to give him ... ways of God.

He often told me:

All that I have heard others say, a... found in books, all that I have written n... ...ns savorless, dull, and heavy when compared ...th what faith has unfolded to me of the unspeakable riches of God and of Jesus Christ.

Christ alone can reveal Himself to us.

We toil and exercise our mind in reason and in science, forgetting that therein we can see only a copy, while we neglect to gaze on the incomparable original.

In the depths of our soul, God reveals Himself, if we but realized it, yet we will not look there for Him.[7]

We leave Him to spend our time in foolish behavior or speech, and pretend to scorn communing with Him, who is ever-present, who is our King.

It is not enough to know God as theory from what we read in books, or feel some fleeting affection for Him that is brief as the wave of feeling or glimpse of the Divine that prompts them.

Our faith must be alive,[8] *and we must make it so, and by its power lift ourselves beyond all these passing emotions to worship the Father and Jesus Christ in all their divine perfection. This path of faith is the spirit of the Church, and will lead to great perfection.*[9]

Not only did Brother Lawrence perceive God as present in his soul by faith,[10] but in all the events of life, whenever

...ey happened, he would instantly arise and seek the presence of God.[11]

A leafless tree that he saw in winter first flashed in upon his soul the fact of God.[12]

The vision was so great and sublime that after forty years it was as clear and vivid as when he first received it. This was his practice throughout his life, using things he saw to lead him up to the Unseen Eternal.

In his reading, Brother Lawrence far preferred the holy Gospels Matthew, Mark, Luke, and John above all other books, since he found that he could nourish his faith more simply and more purely by the very words of Jesus Christ.

Pursuing the Sense of the Presence of God

It was in this way that Brother Lawrence set out upon the spiritual life, with <u>firm resolve</u> and faithful pursuit, to foster in his heart this <u>sublime sense of the presence of God, as seen through faith</u>.

He continued in this without swerving, glorifying God, and showing his love to Him in so many ways they cannot be counted. <u>In everything he did</u> he <u>entreated the aid of our Lord, giving thanks after he had performed his task</u>.

If he felt he had been negligent in his work, he <u>confessed it immediately</u> and asked pardon for it trustfully, without, as he termed it, pleading with God.

Since this communion with God was interwoven with his daily labor, which furnished him with substance for it, he did his work with the greater ease. And very far from distracting him from his communion, <u>his work aided him in it</u>.

Yet he confessed that it was <u>hard at first</u>, that many times he had been unmindful of this practice, but that after <u>humble confession of his failure</u> he had committed himself to it again without concern.

At times a crowd of wandering wild fancies would invade his mind and take violent possession of the place of God. When this happened, he kept quite calm and proceeded immediately to expel them. With this done, he returned to his commune with God.

At last his faithfulness and patience won its reward, in the possession of his soul by a sense, unbroken and undisturbed, of the presence of God.

From that time on, all his many and various activities were changed into an unclouded vision, an illumined love, a joy uninterrupted.

This is what he once told me:

> For me the time of activity does not differ from the time of prayer, and in the noise and clatter of my kitchen, while several persons are together calling for as many different things, I possess God in as great a tranquility as when upon my knees at the blessed Sacrament.[13]

> Sometimes, indeed, my faith becomes so clear[14] that I almost imagine I have lost it. The shadows that usually veil our vision seem to flee away, and there begins to dawn that day which is to be without cloud and without end, the glorious day of the life to come.

To such heights as these, faithfulness led our good brother—faithfulness that directed he cast away all other thoughts and leave his soul free for unbroken communion with God.

In the end, habit became so much second nature that, as he told me, it was in a way impossible for him to turn away from God and busy himself with other matters.

In the "Conversations" he makes an observation on this point that is important. He says that the presence of God can be reached more readily by the heart and by love than by the understanding—these are his words:

> *In the way of God, thoughts count for little, love is everything. Nor is it needful that we should have great things to do.*

I am giving you a picture of a lay brother serving in a kitchen—let me then use his own words.

> *We can do little things for God.*
>
> *I turn the cake that is frying on the pan for the love of Him.*
>
> *When that is done, if there is nothing else to call me I prostrate myself in worship before Him, who has given me grace to work—afterwards, I rise happier than a king.*
>
> *It is enough for me to pick up but a straw from the ground for the love of God.*
>
> *We search for stated ways and methods of learning how to love God, and to come to that love we disquiet our minds by I do not know how many devices.*
>
> *We give ourselves a world of trouble, and pursue a multitude of practices to achieve a sense of the presence of God.*
>
> *Yet it is so simple.*
>
> *How very much shorter and easier it is to do our common business purely for the love of God, to set His consecrating mark on all we lay hands to, and thereby foster the sense of His abiding presence by [constant] communion of our heart with His!*

There is no need either of art or science—we can go to Him just as we are, simply and with single heart.[15] I preserve Brother Lawrence's words religiously, for there is great blessings in them to all who will listen.

We must not imagine, however, that to learn to love God it is enough to offer Him our actions, entreat His aid, and show forth works of love.

Brother Lawrence only attained to the perfection of his love because from the very outset he laid stern discipline upon himself to do nothing that might be displeasing to God, and because he forgot self and renounced all for His sake.

Here are his very words:

Since entering upon the religious life, I no longer perplex myself with thoughts of virtue or of my salvation.[16]

But having given myself wholly to God, to make what satisfaction I could for my sins, and for love of Him having renounced all that is not His, I have come to see that my only business is to live as though there were none but He and I in the world.

Forsaking All of Self
for God

Brother Lawrence began by what was most perfect—forsaking all for God and doing everything for His love. He entirely forgot self. So he no longer thought about heaven or hell or about his past sins, nor about those he daily committed—after he had asked God's forgiveness of them.[17]

Having confessed his sins, he did not allow his mind to go back to them, but, with the confession, entered into perfect peace. After which he commended himself to God, as he used to say, for life and for death, for time and for eternity.

We are made for God, and for Him alone. He cannot, therefore, think it wrong that we forsake all, even ourselves, to find our all in Him.

In God we will see more clearly what we lack than we could in ourselves by all our introspection. In reality, introspection is but the remnant of unexpelled self-love, which, under the guise of zeal for our own perfection, keeps our eyes down on self instead of up to God.

Brother Lawrence often said that during four years of his life,[18] the years of trial, when no one could lift from his soul the burdening sense that he was lost, he had never wavered in his first determination.

29

Instead of vainly attempting to pierce the future, and so vainly dwelling upon the present anguish of his mind, as do most troubled souls, he consoled himself with some such thought as this:

Let what may come of it, however many be the days remaining to me, I will do all things for the love of God.

So by forgetting self, he truly found God.[19]

He told me that in his soul he had found that love for the will of God had taken the place of that which we ordinarily have for our own will.

In all the events of life he saw plainly the workings of the divine will, and this kept him in perfect peace, because his mind was stayed on God.

When he was told of any great wickedness [in the world], he was not a bit surprised, but, he would say, he marveled not to hear of more when he considered the baseness into which sin leads a person.

For his part, he went immediately to the throne of God and prayed and interceded for the sinner. Having done so, he continued in His peace, for He knew that God could remedy any mischief, although He sometimes permitted evil for reasons very true and useful in the order of His providence.[20]

One day I remember telling him, without any forewarning, that a matter of great consequence to him, and one on which he had set his heart and long labored for, could not be carried out, for the superiors had just made up their minds against it.

Quite simply he replied:

We must believe they have good reasons for their decision, and our duty now is to obey and say no more about it.

He did so indeed himself, and although he had many occasions to speak of it afterwards, he did not say one word about it.

Once when Brother Lawrence was very ill, a man questioning the sanctity of life[21] came to visit him and asked him which he would choose if God permitted him—to live a little longer to grow in holiness, or to be received at once into heaven.

The good brother never hesitated, and replied that he would leave the choice to God. As for himself, he said, he had nothing else to do but to wait in peace until God showed him what His will was.

This attitude brought him to so great an indifference about everything, and to such perfect freedom, that it was very like the freedom of the Blessed.

He had no bias, not a trace of self could one discover in his character, and there was no prejudice arising from those natural attachments that people commonly possess.

He was beloved equally by those of most contrary temperaments. He wished well to all, without respect of persons.

He had literally become a true citizen of heaven,[22] and nothing could hold him chained to earth, for his vision was no longer bordered by time.

From long contemplation of Him who is eternal, he had himself become like Him.

Everything came alike to Brother Lawrence, every station, every duty. The good brother found God everywhere, as near when he was at the humblest task as when praying with the [others in the] community.[23]

He found no urgency for retreats,[24] because in the common task he met the same God to love and worship as he did in the stillness of the desert.

Do All for the Love of God

Brother Lawrence's one method of going to God and abiding in His presence was to do all for the love of Him. It was a matter of no consequence to him whether he was employed on one thing or the other, provided that therein he sought God's glory. It was to Him he looked, and not to the work at hand.

He knew that the more he was naturally inclined to oppose the work [he was given to do], the greater and more blessed was the love that made him sacrifice his will to God.

The littleness of the work did not lessen one bit the value of the offering, for God does not consider the greatness of the work, but the love that motivates doing it.

Another quality that could be seen in Brother Lawrence was his singular firmness of mind, which in another walk of life would have been called dauntlessness—it gave proof of a noble soul raised far beyond the fear and hope of all that was not God.

He marveled at nothing, and nothing astonished him or gave him cause for fear. This stability of soul sprung from the same source as did all his other virtues.

The high notion that he had of God, revealed in his heart a perfect picture of his Creator in all His sovereign justice and infinite mercy.

Resting on this, he was assured that God would never deceive him, and would only send such things as were good for him, since on his part he was resolved never to grieve Him, but to do and suffer all for love of Him.

One day I asked him who his director was, and he answered that he had none, and that he believed he needed none.

The rule and office of his state[25] marked out for him his path in outward matters, as the Gospel did the obligation of the inner life of loving God with all his heart. Knowing this, a director did not seem needful, but he had great need of a confessor.[26]

Those who consider no other guidance in the spiritual life but their particular dispositions and feelings, who believe that they have nothing more important to do than to examine themselves as to whether they feel devout or not, can have no stability or any certain rule [of conduct].

This is because our dispositions change continually, sometimes due to our own laziness, and sometimes by the order of God, who varies His gifts toward us according to our needs.

Brother Lawrence kept steadfastly in the way of faith, which never changes.

He was ever steady, for the reason that his one purpose was to carry out the duties of the position where God had placed him, counting nothing commendable but the virtues of that position.

Instead of watching his dispositions or stopping to test the way in which he walked, he fixed his gaze on God alone, the goal[27] of his race,[28] and sped along towards Him by daily acts of meekness and righteousness and love. He set himself to do, rather than to reflect on what to do.

The devotion of Brother Lawrence, resting on this solid base, was not given to fantasies.[29] He was convinced that those that are genuine [real] are most often signs of feebleness in a soul, which is content rather with God's gifts[30] than with Himself.

From the time of his novitiate, there was nothing of this in his conduct, at least nothing was heard or seen of it by those who had his confidence, and to whom he commonly unbosomed[31] himself.

All his days he followed in the footprints of the saints, along the sure and certain path of faith.

He strayed not from the beaten track, which leads to salvation by the practice of those virtues that the church has declared from the beginning[32]—he looked at all else with suspicion.

His great common sense and the light afforded by his simple faith warned him of those sunken rocks that are found in the spiritual life, and on which so many souls become shipwrecked by letting themselves drift along the current of curiosity, and by love of novelty and human guidance.

Yet nothing is easier than to avoid these perils when we seek God alone.

In the matter of religion, what is new needs careful examination, since virtue is not of the number of things that grow slowly to perfection, but, on the contrary, is perfect from the very first.

Brother Lawrence's
Final Days

Prepared by such a life, Brother Lawrence saw death draw near without anxiety or concern.

His patience had been great indeed through all his life, but it grew stronger than ever as he approached the end. He was never in the least fretful, even when he was most wracked with pain.

Joy was plain not only on his face, but still more in his speech—so much so, in fact, that those who visited him were compelled to ask if he was not suffering.

"Forgive me," he replied. "Yes, I do suffer. The pains in my side greatly trouble me, but my spirit is happy and well content."

They asked him, "Suppose God wills that you suffer for ten years, what then?"

"I would suffer," he answered, "not for ten years only, but until the Day of Judgment, if it be God's will. And I would hope that He would continue to aid me with His grace to bear it joyfully."[33]

His one desire was that he might suffer something for the love of God, for all his sins, and finding in his last illness a favorable occasion for suffering in this life, he embraced it heartily.[34]

Purposely he told the brethren to turn him on to his right side, knowing that this position gave great pain, and therefore wished to remain in that position to satisfy his burning desire to suffer.

A brother, who was watching at his bed, wished to relieve him in some measure, but twice he answered, "I thank you, my dear brother, but I beg of you to let me bear just a little for the love of God."

Often in the hour of pain he would cry out with fervor, "My God, I worship Thee in my infirmities. Now, now, I shall have something to bear for Thee—good, be it so, may I suffer and die with Thee."

Then he would repeat those verses of the fifty-first Psalm, "Create in me a clean heart, O God. Cast me not away from Thy presence. Restore unto me the joy of Thy salvation."

As the hour when he was to leave this life drew near, he exclaimed frequently, "Oh, faith, faith"—this was indeed more expressive of his life than any longer utterance could be.

His worship of God never ceased as he approached death. He told a brother of the community[35] that he hardly needed faith any longer to realize God present in his soul, for already faith was nearly swallowed up in sight.

So amazing was his boldness in that dark valley from which so many shrink, that he told one person who had asked him that he feared neither death nor hell, neither the judgment of God nor the attacks of the evil one.

His words were so full of comfort and of grace that many of the brothers questioned him.

One of them asked him if he knew how terrible a thing it was to fall into the hands of the living God,[36] since no man, whoever he be, knows for certain whether he deserves God's love or not.[37]

"I agree," said Brother Lawrence, "but I should not wish to know it for fear of vanity—we can do nothing better than abandon ourselves to God."

After he had received the last sacraments,[38] a brother asked him if he were at ease and what his mind was occupied with.

This was his reply: "I am doing what I shall do through all eternity—blessing God, praising God, adoring God, giving Him the love of my whole heart.

"It is our one business, my brothers, to worship Him and love Him without thought of anything else."

One of the community commended himself to Brother Lawrence's prayers, and begged him to entreat God that he be given the true spirit of prayer.

Brother Lawrence replied that there was need of labor on the brother's part also to make himself worthy of such a gift.[39]

These were his last words.

The next day, which was Monday, February 12, 1691, at nine o'clock in the morning, without any pain or struggle, without losing the slightest use of any of his faculties, Brother Lawrence passed away in the embrace of his Lord, and rendered his soul to God in the peace and calm of one who had fallen asleep.

Part of the Great Band Who Have Forsaken the World for Christ

Nothing can give a clearer picture of a true Christian philosophy in practice than the life and death of Brother Lawrence. He was part of that great band who from times of old have forsaken the world to dedicate with single heart their powers to cultivate the life of the spirit, and to come to a knowledge of God and of His Son Jesus Christ. Those devoted souls who have taken the Gospel as their only rule and have faithfully professed the holy philosophy of the cross.

In St. Clement of Alexandria's description of such people in the Seventh Book of the Stromata,[39] it would seem that he had in view a person just like Brother Lawrence when he said that the great business of a philosopher, that is, a wise Christian, is prayer.

Such people pray in every place, at every time, not using many words or thinking to be heard for their much speaking,[40] but in secret in the depths of their soul[41]—while walking, conversing with others, reading, eating, or working.

Their praises rise to God unceasingly—not only at specific times during the day, but in all their actions they glorify God as do the seraphim.[42]

Continual contemplation through prayer on spiritual things makes them meek, gentle, patient, and yet strong as iron to battle with temptation and allow it no hold upon themselves, either of pleasure or of sorrow.

The joy of contemplation on which they feed unceasingly, without being excessively satisfied, renders them indifferent to all empty pleasures.

They dwell by love with God, and having seen through faith a vision of the Light of lights, they have no taste for what the world can offer.

Through love they have attained already what they lack and they long for nothing, because, so far as they can in this life, they have the object of their heart's desire.

They have no ground for fear, since nothing in this life can hurt them or turn their heart from the love of God.

They have no need to train their spirit to be calm, for their mind is at rest because they are persuaded that all things work together for good.[43]

Nothing disturbs them, and they do not know anger because of the love they have for God. Jealousy can gain no entrance, since they lack nothing.

They love others with no mere human fondness, but as the objects of the love of a loved and loving Father. Their spirit is steadfast and unchangeable, for they have committed all their ways unto God and rest on Him alone.

I should like to add to this portrait a finishing touch from the hand of a great master—a person who was more illumined by the light of the faith that he had in common with Brother Lawrence than by all the science and philosophy of Greece.

Will anyone find fault with me for ranking together the great masters and doctors with an obscure lay brother, when we find in his simple words and life the same full purity and perfection of Christian precept and practice that the greatest lights of the Church have handed down to us?[44]

All alike have drawn from Jesus Christ, who hides Himself from those who in their own imaginations are wise and prudent, and reveals Himself to the humble and lowly of heart.

No one can be more brave or dauntless, says Saint Gregory of Nazianzus[45] ("Orat. 28"),[46] than true Christian philosophers. Everything gives way to their largeness of heart.

If they are denied all that the earth can give, they have wings with which to fly and find their refuge in God. They know no limits—they live on earth as people wholly in heaven, unmoved amid the storm of passions.

They yield in everything, except in the greatness of their courage, and by yielding they surpass those who wish to outshine them.

They use the supports of life ("Orat. 29") no further than necessity obliges them. Their only intercourse is with God.

Raised above all things of outward sense, their soul is a stainless, spotless, mirror, reflecting the divine without any intermingling of what is gross and earthly.

Daily they add new lights of virtue to those they already have, until at length they come unto Him, who is the Fountain of Light.

In His light they will indeed see light when the Glory of Truth will have scattered the darkness of all enigmas in that day of perfect bliss.

(In these words of Saint Gregory of Nazianzus, we can easily recognize our lay brother and all those of like mind and heart.)

Though it was in a very lowly corner that Brother Lawrence lived his days, yet there is no person, of whatever station or condition they may be, who cannot draw great profit from his life.

Those who are filled with the cares of this world he will teach to draw near to God, to ask from Him the grace to do their duty faithfully.

He will teach them never to forget that they can approach God when they are the most busy, wherever they are and whatever they are doing, and during their times of leisure.

By the example of our good brother, they will be moved to render thanks to God for all His mercies and for the good that He inspires them to do, humbling themselves before Him for their many failures.

In the pages of this book they will not find set out for them a devotion that is merely speculative, or that can only be practiced in an isolated or secret place.

There is an obligation laid on every person to worship God and love Him.

We cannot carry out this solemn duty as we should unless our heart is knit in love to God, and our communion[47] with Him is so close as to compel us to run to Him at every moment, just like little children who cannot stand upright without their mother's arms of love.

Far from this communion with our Father being difficult, it is very easy and very necessary for every one—it is to this that the apostle Paul says all Christians are obliged.[48]

Whoever does not practice it, whoever does not feel their great necessity, whoever does not grasp their total inability to do it correctly alone,[49] is ignorant of their own self, ignorant of God their Father, utterly ignorant of their continual need of Jesus Christ.

No affairs or cares of the world can serve as an excuse for neglecting this our duty.

God is everywhere, in all places, and there is no spot where we cannot draw near to Him and hear Him speaking in our heart. With a little love, just a very little, we will not find it hard.

Those that are withdrawn from the embarrassments and perplexities of life have even greater opportunities of following in the steps of Brother Lawrence.[50]

Freed for the most part from the ambitions and conventions of the world, which give to those who must be active in it most of their cares and troubles, there is nothing to hinder them from taking the example of Brother Lawrence and renouncing all desire other than that of living every moment of their life, and doing every action, for the love of God.

Thus giving to Him—in Brother Lawrence's own words—"the all for the all."

The example of his complete detachment from the world, of his entire forgetfulness of self, which led him to think no longer even of his salvation to keep his mind free for God to fill, of his indifference to what life might bring, and of his freedom in the spiritual life, cannot fail to be filled with blessing beyond measure.

"Believe me," said Brother Lawrence, "count as lost each day you have not used in loving God."

Endnotes

1   The author is probably M. Beaufort, grand vicar to M. de Chalons, Cardinal de Noailles, the same person who compiled the conversations and correspondence with Brother Lawrence.

2   Carmelites (called White Friars in England), were a mendicant order of "Our Lady of Mount Carmel." The original order claimed the prophet Elijah as its founder, but now it is believed to have been founded in the middle of the 12th century, about 1155. In a mendicant order, the friars were forbidden to hold personal or community property, and supported themselves by working or begging—more the latter than the former. Lawrence was not a friar, but a brother, which is a member of a male religious order for laypeople who engage in the service of the order, but not in the holy vows.

3   John 10:1-9

4   Matthew 11:28-30

5   No copy of the "Life" of Brother Lawrence seems to have survived, but the "Letters" are part of this book.

6   page 41

7   Ephesians 3:17

8   Hebrews 11:6

9   page 42

10   Ephesians 3:17

11   Psalm 14:2, 22:26, 27:8

12   page 41

13   page 61

14   Free from what dims, obscures, or darkens; unclouded.

15   page 52

16   page 45

17   1 John 1:9

18   page 51

19 bid

20 page 42

21 The man was François de Salignac de La Mothe Fénelon (1651-1715), Archbishop of Cambrai, France, a contemporary and close friend of Madame Jeanne Guyon, and author of *Spiritual Letters and Maxims of the Saints*. In 1699, Pope Innocent XII condemned parts of the latter book for Fénelon's views and approval of the contemplative life. Soon after, both upon the urging of the pope and because he was offended by Fénelon's novel *Télémaque* (1699), which he considered to be a satire of his court, Louis XIV exiled Fénelon to his diocese. See *The Foxes Book of Martyrs*, and *Experiencing Union with God through Inner Prayer* and *The Way and Results of that Union* by Madame Jeanne Guyon, both published by Bridge-Logos Publishers in their Pure Gold Classics series.

22 John 15:19, 17:14-16; Hebrews 11:13; 1 Peter 2:11

23 page 48

24 If alive today, Brother Lawrence would undoubtedly feel the same way about the many camp meetings and conferences held each year, especially in the spring and summer, that many attend to find the presence and power of God.

25 His main duties included work first as a cook and later as a sandal maker.

26 The same person sometimes held the office of director and the office of confessor, therefore, the terms are sometimes used synonymously. Strictly speaking, however, it was not the business of the director to hear confession but simply to give religious counsel when Christians, especially in the beginning of their religious life, needed it.

27 Philippians 3:14

28 Acts 20:24; 1 Corinthians 9:24; 2 Timothy 4:7; Hebrews 12:1

29 *Fantasies* probably refers to visions. A now obsolete meaning of fantasy is hallucination. Acts 2:17; 2 Corinthians 12:1

30 1 Corinthians 12

31 *Unbosom*: to confide one's thoughts or feelings. To relieve oneself of troublesome thoughts or feelings. To reveal one's thoughts or feelings.

32 The statement, "virtues that the church has declared from the beginning," refers to the traditions and beliefs of the Roman Catholic church, not necessarily the Church universal.

33 This section is based upon the belief that physical pain, in and of itself, has a redeeming quality, and when offered to God is accepted by Him as some measure of payment for sins. It is true that we are called to suffer for Christ's sake, to suffer in His name, to suffer persecution, to suffer for righteousness—and this often involves physical suffering, but He suffered fully for our sins and no further suffering for them is required, or accepted, by God on our part. For Him to do so would denigrate the suffering of His Son, who was sent to suffer for us, and by His suffering and death reconcile us to God. (Acts 5:41, 9:16, 17:3, 26:3; Romans 5:10, 2 Corinthians 5:18, Philippians 1:29; Colossians 1:19-20-22; 2 Timothy 3:12; Hebrews 2:9, 9:26; James 5:13-14; 1 Peter 2:19, 3:14)

34 The community would be those who lived in the monastery of the barefooted Carmelites at Paris.

35 Hebrews 10:31

36 Notwithstanding, God's love for us now and forever in Christ is guaranteed on the strength and truth of His Word. (Romans 5:8, 8:37-39; Galatians 2:20; Ephesians 2:4, 3:19, 5:2; 2 Thessalonians 2:16; James 2:5; 1 John 3:1, 4:7-12, 16, 19)

37 This is the sacrament of "Extreme Unction," which was a rite in which a priest anointed and prayed for a sick or an injured person, especially one in danger of death. In 1972 the name and rite were changed to "Anointing of the Sick." It is probably based on James 5:14,15, which scripturally is a prayer and anointing that the universal Church is supposed to administer to the sick for healing, and not a prayer for the dying.

38 1 Corinthians 2:12, 12:11

39 New Advent, Church Fathers, http://www.newadvent.org/fathers/02107.htm

40 Matthew 6:7

41 This is the form of prayer that Madame Jeanne Guyon, who lived during the time of Lawrence and Fénelon, referred to as "inner prayer." See the Pure Gold Classic, *Experiencing Union with God through Inner Prayer* and *The Way and Results of that Union*, published by Bridge-Logos Publishers.

42 Isaiah 6:3

43 Romans 8:28

44 Although this statement is meant to refer specifically to those within the particular denomination to which Brother Lawrence belonged, it easily broadens to include all the holy men and women of the universal Church of our Lord.

45 Saint Gregory of Nazianzus, (329?-389?), a churchman whose writings contain the best statement of the doctrine of the Trinity in Greek Orthodox theology. His festival is held each year on May 9.

46 No major encyclopedia, dictionary, or quotation reference recognized this abbreviation, and no quotations attributed to Saint Gregory of Nazianzus could be found.

47 *Communion*: In this context it means religious or spiritual fellowship.

48 Uncertain as to exact statement of Paul to which this refers. (1 Corinthians 1:9; 2 Corinthians 13:14; Ephesians 6:18; Philippians 4:6; Colossians 4:2; 1 Thessalonians 5:17; 1 Timothy 2:8)

49 Romans 8:26

50 Although this undoubtedly refers to those living a monastic life, it equally applies to Christian couples who have retired from work, to older widows and widowers, and to any whose outside activities are restrained temporarily or permanently for any reason. Many revivals of the Church have come from the prayers of elderly, and often ill or disabled, women who spent their hours communicating

4

III
Conversations with Brother Lawrence

First Conversation

The first time I saw Brother Lawrence was on August 3, 1666.[1] During our conversation he told me many things—among them, that God had done him a remarkable favor in his conversion at age eighteen.

That winter, seeing a tree stripped of its leaves, and considering that within a little time the leaves would be renewed and the flowers and fruit would appear, he received a high view of the providence and power of God that had never left his soul.

This view perfectly set him loose from the world, and kindled in him such a great love for God that he could not tell whether it had increased during the more than forty years since then.

He had been footman to M. Fieubert, the treasurer—and he himself was a great awkward fellow who broke everything.

He had desired to be accepted into a monastery, thinking that he should be made to suffer there for his awkwardness and the faults he would commit,[2] and so he felt he should sacrifice his life and its pleasures to God. But God had disappointed him, for he had met with nothing but satisfaction in that state.

We should establish ourselves in a sense of God's presence by continually conversing with Him.[3] It is a shameful thing to stop conversing with God to think of unimportant things and foolishness.

We should feed and nourish our souls with high notions of God, which would yield us great joy in being devoted to Him. We should quicken—that is, enliven—our faith.

It is lamentable that we have so little,[4] and that instead of taking faith for the rule of conduct, people amuse themselves with trivial devotions that change daily.

The way of faith is the spirit of the Church,[5] and it is sufficient to bring us to a high degree of perfection.[6]

We should give ourselves completely to God in both temporal and spiritual things, and seek our satisfaction only in the fulfilling of His will, whether He leads us by suffering or by consolation, for both are equal to a soul truly resigned.

There needs to be fidelity in those times of dryness or insensibility and irksomeness in prayer, by which God tries our love to Him.

That is the time for us to make good and effectual acts of resignation, for often one act alone will highly promote our spiritual advancement.

Concerning the miseries and sins in the world that Brother Lawrence heard of daily, he was so far from wondering at them that, on the contrary, he was surprised there were not more, considering the malice sinners were capable of.

As for his part, he prayed for them, but troubled himself no further, for he knew that God could remedy the mischief they did when He pleased.

In order to arrive at such resignation as God requires, we should watch attentively over all the passions that mingle as much in spiritual things as in those of a grosser nature.[7]

To those who truly desire to serve Him, God will give light concerning those passions.

Brother Lawrence ended the conversation by saying that if it was my intention to serve God sincerely, I could come to him as often as I pleased, without any fear of being troublesome. But if it was not my intention, then I should not visit him anymore.

Second Conversation

September 28, 1666

During our second conversation, Brother Lawrence said that he had always been governed by love, without selfish views, and that having resolved to make the love of God the end of all his actions, he had found reasons to be well satisfied with his method.

He was pleased when he could take up a straw from the ground for the love of God, seeking Him only and nothing else, not even His gifts.[8]

He had been long troubled in mind from a certain belief that he should be damned, and that all the people in the world could not have persuaded him to the contrary, but he had finally reasoned with himself about it in this way:

I engaged in a religious life only for the love of God, and I have endeavored to act only for Him. Whatever becomes of me, whether I be lost or saved, I will always continue to act purely for the love of God. I shall have this good at least, that until death I shall have done all that is in me to love Him.

This trouble of mind lasted four years, during which time he suffered much. At last, however, he saw that this trouble arose from lack of faith, and since then he has passed his life in perfect liberty and continual joy.[9] He had placed his sins between him and God, as it were, to tell Him that he did not deserve His favors, but that God still continued to bestow them in abundance.

In order to form a habit of conversing with God continually and referring all we do to Him, we must first apply ourselves diligently to Him. After a little careful attention, however, we will find His love inwardly exciting us to it without any difficulty.

After the pleasant days God had given him, Brother Lawrence expected that he would have his turn of pain and suffering.

But he was not uneasy about it, knowing very well that since he could do nothing of himself, God would not fail to give Him the strength to bear it.

When an occasion of practicing some virtue was offered, he addressed himself to God by saying, "Lord, I cannot do this unless You enable me."

Having done so, he would then receive more than sufficient strength.[10]

When he failed in his duty, he only confessed his fault, saying to God, "I shall never do otherwise if You leave me to myself—it is You who must prevent my falling and repair what is defective in me."

After that, he gave himself no further uneasiness about it.

We should act with God in the greatest simplicity, speaking to Him frankly and plainly, and imploring His assistance in our affairs when and in the manner they take place.

God never fails to grant it, as Brother Lawrence had often experienced.

Recently he had been sent into Burgundy to buy the provision of wine for the society, which was a very unwelcome task for him, for he had no skill for business and was lame and could not go about the boat except by rolling himself over the casks.

He gave himself no uneasiness about it, however, or about the purchase of the wine.

He said to God it was His business he was about, and afterward found it very well performed.

The year before he had been sent into Auvergne for the same reason, and though he could not tell how the matter proceeded, it turned out well.[11]

It was the same in his business in the kitchen, to which he had a natural and great aversion. Having accustomed himself to do everything there for the love of God, he prayed on all occasions for His grace to do his work well,[12] and thus found everything easy during the fifteen years he had been employed there.[13]

He was well pleased with the post he was now in, but was as ready to give up this one as the former one,[14] since by doing little things for the love of God he was always pleasing to himself in every condition.

For him, the set times of prayer were not different from other times. He retired to pray when directed by his superior, but that he did not want such retirement nor ask for it, because his greatest business did not divert him from God.

Since he knew his obligation to love God in all things, and since he constantly endeavored to do so, he had no need of a director to advise him, but he much needed a confessor to absolve him.[15]

He was very sensible of his faults, but not discouraged by them. He did not plead to God to excuse his sins, but simply confessed them to Him.[16] When he had done so, he peaceably resumed his usual practice of love and adoration.

During the time when his mind was troubled he had consulted no one. Knowing only by the light of faith that God was present,[17] he contented himself with directing all his actions to Him—that is, did them with a desire to please Him, and allowing whatever would to come of it.[18]

Useless thoughts spoil everything, and mischief begins there.[19] We should reject such thoughts as soon as we perceive their uselessness to the matter at hand, or to our salvation, and return to our communion with God.

In the beginning he had often passed his time appointed for prayer in rejecting wandering thoughts and immediately falling back into them.

He could never regulate his devotion by using certain methods as some do. At first he had meditated [during prayer] for some time, but afterward that stopped in a way [or for some reason] that he could not remember.

All bodily mortification[20] and other exercises are useless, except as they serve to arrive at a union with God by love.

He had well considered this, and found that the shortest way is to go straight to God by a continual exercise of love[21] and doing all things for His sake.[22]

We should recognize the great difference between the acts of the understanding and those of the will—the first are of comparatively little value, and the second are everything.

Our only business is to love and delight ourselves in God.[23]

All possible kinds of mortification, if they are without the love of God, cannot erase a single sin.

We should, without anxiety, expect the pardon [cleansing] of our sins by the blood of Jesus Christ,[24] only endeavoring to love Him with all our hearts.

God seemed to have granted the greatest favors to the greatest sinners as more notable monuments of His mercy.

The greatest pains or pleasures of this world were not to be compared with what he had experienced of both kinds in a spiritual state.

Consequently, he was careful for nothing and feared nothing, desiring only one thing of God—namely, that he might not offend Him.

He had no scruples.[25]

"For when I fail in my duty," he said, "I readily acknowledge it, saying, 'I am used to doing so, and I will never do otherwise if I am left to myself.' If I do not fail, then I give God thanks, acknowledging that the strength comes from Him."[26]

Third Conversation

November 22, 1666

Brother Lawrence told me that the foundation of the spiritual life in him was a high notion and esteem of God in faith.

Once he had well conceived those [established them within himself], he had no other concern at first [in the beginning] but to reject faithfully every other thought—so that he might perform all his actions for the love of God.

When sometimes he had not thought of God for quite awhile, he did not disquiet himself [become anxious] because of it.

But after acknowledging his wretchedness to God, he returned to Him with much greater trust in Him than the misery he caused himself through forgetting Him.[27]

The trust we put in God honors Him much and draws down great graces.

It is not only impossible that God would deceive, but also that He would let a soul that is perfectly resigned to Him, and resolved to endure everything for His sake, suffer for long.

He had so often experienced the ready assistance of divine grace upon all occasions that, based upon those experiences, when he had business to do he did not think of it beforehand.

When it was time to do it, he found in God, as in a clear mirror, all that was suitable [or necessary] for him to do.

Lately he had acted that way without anticipating care,[28] but before the experiences mentioned above, he had used it [anticipating care] in his affairs.

When outward business diverted him a little from the thought of God, a fresh remembrance would come from God and envelop his soul, and so inflame and transport him that it was difficult for him to contain himself.

He was more united to God in his outward activities than when he left them for devotion and retirement.

He expected hereafter[29] some great pain of body or mind, and that the worst that could happen to him was to lose that sense of God that he had enjoyed so long.

But the goodness of God assured him He would not forsake him utterly,[30] and that He would give him strength to bear whatever evil He permitted to happen to him.[31]

He feared nothing, therefore, and had no need to consult with anybody about his state. When he had attempted to do it [consult with somebody], he always came away more perplexed.

Because he was conscious of his readiness to lay down his life for the love of God, he had no apprehension of danger. Perfect resignation to God is a sure way to heaven, a way in which he always had sufficient light for his conduct.[32]

In the beginning of the spiritual life we should be faithful in doing our duty and denying ourselves. [After Brother Lawrence did that], unspeakable pleasures followed.

In difficulties we need only have recourse to Jesus Christ and beseech His grace—with that, everything becomes easy.

Many do not advance in Christian progress because they stick in penances and particular exercises[33] while neglecting the love of God, which must be the end purpose of all actions.

This is shown plainly by their works, and is the reason why we see so little solid virtue [in them].

Neither art nor science is needed for going to God, but only a heart resolutely determined to apply itself to nothing but Him, or for His sake, and to love Him only.

Fourth Conversation

November 25, 1666

Brother Lawrence talked with me frequently, and with great openness of heart, about his way of going to God, some of which I've related already.

All consists in one hearty renunciation of everything that we realize does not lead to God, so that we might accustom ourselves to a continual conversation with Him, with freedom and in simplicity.

We need only to recognize that God is intimately present with us to address ourselves to Him every moment. Thus we may [continually] beseech His assistance in knowing His will in doubtful things, and for rightly performing those that we plainly see He requires of us—offering them to Him before we do them, and giving Him thanks when we have done them.

In this conversation with God, we should also be active in praising, adoring, and loving Him incessantly for His infinite goodness and perfection.

Without being discouraged on account of our sins, we should pray for His grace with perfect confidence—by relying upon the infinite merits of our Lord Jesus Christ.

God never fails to offer us His grace at each action.

Brother Lawrence distinctly perceived it and never failed for lack of it, except when his thoughts wandered from a sense of God's presence, or he forgot to ask [for] His assistance.

God always gives us light in [the midst of] our doubts when we have no other design but to please Him.

Our sanctification does not depend upon changing our works, but in doing for God's sake what we normally do for our own.

It is lamentable to see how many people mistake the means for the end,[34] addicting themselves to certain works that they perform very imperfectly because of their human or selfish regards.

The most excellent method he had found of going to God was that of doing our common business without any view of pleasing people,[35] and—as far we are capable—purely for the love of God.

It is a great delusion to think that the times of prayer should differ from other times. We are as strictly obliged to adhere to God by action in the time of action as by prayer in the time of prayer.

His prayer was nothing else but a sense of the presence of God, his soul being at that time insensible to everything but divine love.

When the appointed times of prayer were past, he found no difference, because he still continued with God, praising and blessing Him with all his might.

Consequently, he passed his life in continual joy—yet hoped that God would give him something to suffer when he grew stronger.

We should, once and for all, heartily put our whole trust in God and make a total surrender of ourselves to Him, secure [in the knowledge] that He will not deceive us.[36]

We should not grow weary of doing little things for the love of God, who considers not the greatness of the work, but the love with which it is performed.[37]

We should not be surprised if in the beginning we often fail in our [spiritual] endeavors, but eventually we should develop a habit that will naturally produce its [victorious] acts in us without our care,[38] and to our exceeding great delight.

The whole substance of religion is faith, hope, and charity [love],[39] by whose practice we become united to the will of God.

All things besides these are indifferent [do not matter], and are to be used as a means whereby we may arrive at our objective, and be swallowed up therein by faith and charity [love].

All things are possible to those who believe, less difficult to those who hope, more easy to those who love, and still more easy to those who persevere in the practice of these three virtues.

The end we should propose to ourselves is to become in this life the most perfect worshipers of God we can possibly be, just as we hope to be through all eternity.

When we enter upon the spiritual life, we should consider and examine thoroughly what we are. Having done that, we will find ourselves worthy of all contempt and, in truth, not deserving the name of Christians. As such, we are subject to all kinds of misery and numberless accidents that trouble us and cause perpetual vicissitudes [changes] in our health, in our humors,[40] in our internal and external dispositions.

In fine,[41] persons whom God would humble by many pains and labors, as well within as without.

After this we should not be surprised that troubles, temptations, oppositions, and contradictions happen to us from people.

We should, on the contrary, submit ourselves to them—and bear them as long as God pleases—as things that are highly advantageous to us.

The greater the perfection a soul aspires after, the more dependent it is upon divine grace.

Other Accounts of Brother Lawrence

Being questioned by one of his own society—to whom he was obliged to open himself—by what means he had attained such an habitual sense of [the presence of] God, Brother Lawrence told him that since his first coming to the monastery he had considered God as the end of all his thoughts and desires, as the mark toward which they should move, and in which they should terminate.

In the beginning of his novitiate,[42] he spent the hours appointed for private prayer in thinking of God, so as to convince his mind of the divine existence and impress it deeply upon his heart.

This he desired to do by devout sentiments and submission to the lights of faith, rather than by studied reasonings[43] and elaborate meditations.

By this short and sure method he exercised himself in the knowledge and love of God, resolving to use his utmost endeavor to live in a continual sense of His presence, and, if possible, never to forget Him anymore.

When he had thus in prayer filled his mind with great sentiments of that infinite Being, he went to his work appointed in the kitchen—he was cook to the society.

There, having first considered the different things his office required, and when and how each thing was to be done, he spent all the intervals of his time, as well as before and after his task, in prayer.

When he began his work, he said to God, with a filial trust in Him:

O my God, since Thou art with me, and I must now, in obedience to Thy commands, apply my mind to these outward things, I beseech Thee to grant me the grace to continue in Thy presence; and to this end do Thou prosper me with Thy assistance, receive all my works, and possess all my affections.

As he proceeded in his work, he continued his familiar conversation with his Maker, imploring His grace, and offering to Him all his actions.[44]

When he had finished, he examined himself how he had discharged his duty.

If he found [he had done it] well, he returned thanks to God.

If otherwise, he asked pardon and, without being discouraged, he set his mind right again, and continued his exercise of the presence of God as if he had never deviated from it.

By rising after my falls, and by frequently renewed acts of faith and love, I have come to a state wherein it would be as difficult for me not to think of God as it was at first to accustom myself to it.

Because Brother Lawrence had found such an advantage in walking in the presence of God, it was natural for him to recommend it earnestly to others, but his example was a stronger inducement than any arguments he could propose.

His very countenance was edifying—such a sweet and calm devotion appearing in it as could not but affect the beholders.

It was also observed that in the greatest hurry of business in the kitchen he still preserved his recollection and heavenly mindedness.

He was never hasty nor loitering, but did each thing in its season, with an even, uninterrupted composure and tranquility of spirit.

My time of business, is no different with me from the time of prayer. In the noise and clatter of my kitchen, while several people are at the same time calling for different things, I possess God in as great tranquility as if I were upon my knees at the blessed sacrament.[45]

Endnotes

1 Brother Lawrence would have been 52 years old at this time, having been born in 1614.

2 Based upon a belief that suffering itself has redemptive qualities.

3 1 Thessalonians 5:17

4 Matthew 6:30; Matthew 8:26, 14:31, 16:8, 17:20; Luke 12:28

5 Romans 5:1; Ephesians 2:8-9

6 Hebrews 6:1

7 Proverbs 4:23; Matthew 15:19-20; Mark 7:21-23

8 For an in-depth study of love, see *The Greatest Thing in the World* by Henry Drummond, a Pure Gold Classic published by Bridge-Logos Publishers.

9 Romans 5:16-19, 8:1

10 Philippians 4:13

11 Proverbs 16:3

12 Hebrews 4:16

13 There is no indication of how long it was between the first and second conversation, but it is doubtful that it was fifteen years, for Brother Lawrence would then be seventy and not likely to be rolling over wine casks on a boat.

14 This undoubtedly was when Brother Lawrence was a sandal maker, so the former post or occupation that he refers to would have been when he was a cook in the monastery kitchen.

15 *Absolve*: to grant a remission of sin to—to pardon or remit (a sin). Based on a doctrine in some churches that sins must be confessed to a person holding a particular religious office to be forgiven. Probably taken from James 5:16—"Therefore confess your faults one to another, and pray for one another, that ye may be healed. The effectual fervent prayer of a righteous man availeth much."

16 1 John 1:19—Considering Brother Lawrence's belief that he needed a confessor, he probably regarded confessing his sins to his confessor as confessing them to God—by way of the confessor.

17 Hebrews 11:6

18 1 Corinthians 10:31; Colossians 3:23

19 Mark 7:21

20 *Mortification*: discipline of the body and the appetites by self-denial or self-inflicted privation.

21 1 Corinthians 13:13

22 2 Corinthians 4:5, 11, 5:13, 12:10; Philippians 3:7-8; Hebrews 11:26; 1 Peter 2:13

23 Matthew 22:36-38

24 Ephesians 2:13; Hebrews 9:14; 1 Peter 1:18-19; 1 John 1:7

25 *Scruple*: an uneasy feeling arising from conscience or principle that tends to hinder action.

26 Habakkuk 3:19; Philippians 4:13; 2 Timothy 4:17; 1 Peter 4:11

27 The "much greater trust" was not as a result of forgetting God, but deliberate and determined trust for having forgotten Him.

28 In this sentence, *anticipating* probably means "in advance" or "beforehand," and care probably means "caution" or "calculation." Lawrence seems to be saying that prior to developing trust in God's assistance in all his affairs, he planned in advance exactly what he was going to do, but that he no longer did that.

29 It is not clear what previous event "hereafter" refers to— perhaps to the blessings Lawrence sometimes experienced. Brother Lawrence seemed to believe that blessings from God were always followed by suffering from God, which was a peculiar doctrine of his church.

30 Hebrews 13:5

31 Philippians 4:13

32 The original last part of this sentence in all the versions we examined read: " ... a way in which he always had sufficient light for our conduct." Obviously, however, the "he" and the "our" do not go together. So the last part of the sentence should read either as we now have it, which seems the most correct, or: "... a way in which we always have sufficient light for our conduct." There is also a slight possibility, of course, that the original way is correct, but that the "he" should be capitalized to indicate that the "He" is God.

33 *Exercises* are activities that require spiritual and mental exertion, especially when intended to develop or maintain spiritual growth.

34 The work itself rather than the objective, or end purpose, of God's glory.

35 Galatians 1:10; Ephesians 6:5-6

36 Titus 1:1-2

37 Galatians 6:9

38 Care has several definitions that would apply here: a burdened state of mind, as that arising from heavy responsibilities; worry; an object or source of worry, attention, or solicitude; close attention; painstaking application.

39 1 Corinthians 13:13

40 *Humors*: Probably refers to one of the four fluids of the body, blood, phlegm, choler, and black bile, whose relative proportions were thought in ancient physiology to determine a person's disposition and general health.

41 In this usage, *fine* means in conclusion, in summation, or in brief.

42 *Novitiate*: The period of being a novice.

43 *Studied reasonings*: Conclusions, inferences, or judgments resulting from deliberation and careful thought.

44 Philippians 4:6-7

45 Receiving the Eucharist—communion.

IV
Letters of
Brother Lawrence

Brother Lawrence wrote these letters
to members in his religious order, their friends,
and his friends. Though addressed to specific people,
since their publication after his death,
they have encouraged believers for centuries
to walk in the presence of God.

This collection of Brother Lawrence's letters
has been organized into chronological order.
The original publishers kept the addressees
anonymous.

First Letter

June 1, 1682

My Dearest Prioress,[1]

I have taken this opportunity to communicate to you the sentiments of one of our society, concerning the admirable effects and continual assistances that he receives from the presence of God. Let you and me both profit by them.

You must know his continual care has been, for about the past forty years that he has spent in religion, to be always with God, and to do nothing, say nothing, and think nothing that may displease Him. This without any other view than purely for the love of Him,[2] and because He deserves infinitely more. He is now so accustomed to that divine presence, that he receives from it continual assistance upon all occasions.

For about thirty years his soul has been filled with joys so continual, and sometimes so great, that he is forced to use means to moderate them, and to hinder their appearing outwardly.

If sometimes he is a little too much absent from that divine presence, God presently makes Himself felt in his soul to recall him, which often happens when he is most engaged in his outward business. He answers with exact fidelity to these inward drawings, either by an elevation of his heart toward God, or by a meek and fond regard for Him. Or by such words as love forms upon these occasions—for instance, "My God, here I am all devoted to Thee. Lord, make me according to Thy heart."

Then it seems to him (as in effect he feels it) that this God of love, satisfied with such few words, reposes again, and rests in the wellspring and center of his soul.

The experience of these things gives him such an assurance that God is always in the source or wellspring of his soul that it renders him incapable of doubting it for any reason whatever.

Judge by this what contentment and satisfaction he enjoys while he continually finds in himself so great a treasure. He is no longer on an anxious search for it, but has it open before him, and he may take what he pleases of it.

He complains much of our blindness, and cries often that we who content ourselves with so little are to be pitied.

God, says he, has infinite treasure to bestow, and we are satisfied with a little sensible devotion, which passes in a moment. Blind as we are, we hinder God and stop the current of His graces. But when He finds a soul penetrated with a lively faith, He pours into it His graces and favors plentifully. There they flow like a torrent that has found a passage, after being forcibly stopped against its ordinary course, and spreads itself with impetuosity and abundance.

Yes, we often stop this torrent by the little value we set upon it. But let us stop it no more. Let us enter into ourselves and break down the bank that hinders it. Let us make way for grace. Let us redeem the lost time, for perhaps we have but little left. Death follows us closely. Let us be well prepared for it, for we die but once, and a miscarriage there is irretrievable.

I say again, let us enter into ourselves. The time presses, there is no room for delay—our souls are at stake. I believe you have taken such effectual measures that you will not be surprised. I commend you for it—it is the one thing necessary. We must, nevertheless, always work at it, because not to advance in the spiritual life is to go back. But those who have the gale of the Holy Spirit[3] go forward even in sleep. If the vessel of our soul is still tossed with winds and storms, let us awake the Lord, who reposes in it, and He will quickly calm the sea.[4]

I have taken the liberty to impart to you these good sentiments so that you may compare them with your own. It will serve again to kindle and inflame them, if by misfortune (which God forbid, for it would be indeed a great misfortune) they should be, though ever so little, cooled. Let us, therefore, both recall our first fervency. Let us profit by the example and the sentiments of this brother, who is little known by the world, but known by God and extremely caressed by Him.

I will pray for you. Pray instantly for me, also. I am, in our Lord;

Yours ...

Second Letter

Before November 3, 1685

Reverend ...

I have not found my manner of life in books, although I have no difficulty about it, but for greater [spiritual] security I will be glad to know your thoughts concerning it.

In a conversation some days ago with a person of piety, he told me the spiritual life was a life of grace that begins with servile fear, is increased by hope of eternal life, and is consummated by pure love. Each of these states has its different stages, he said, by which one arrives at last at that blessed fulfillment.

I have not followed all these methods. On the contrary, although I do not know for what reasons, I found they discouraged me.

This was the reason why, at my entrance into religion, I took a resolution to give myself up to God as the best return I could make for His love, and to renounce all for the love of Him.[5]

For the first year, I commonly employed myself during the time set apart for devotion with the thought of death, judgment, heaven, hell, and my sins.

I continued this way for some years, applying my mind carefully the rest of the day, and even in the midst of my business, to the presence of God, whom I considered always as with me, and often as in me.

At length, without effort I began to do the same thing during my set time of prayer, which caused in me great delight and consolation. This practice produced in me so high an esteem for God that faith alone was capable of satisfying me in that point.[6]

Such was my beginning, and yet I must tell you that for the first ten years I suffered much. The fearful thought that I was not devoted to God as I wished to be, my past sins being always present in my mind, and the great unmerited favors that God did for me, were the matter and source of my sufferings.

During this time I fell often, and rose again presently. It seemed to me that all creatures, reason, and God Himself were against me,[7] and faith alone for me.

I was troubled sometimes with thoughts that to believe I had received such favors was the result of my presumption, which pretended to be at once where others arrive with difficulty.

At other times, I felt that it was a willful delusion, and that there was no salvation for me.

When I thought of nothing but to spend my life in these troubles (which did not at all diminish the trust I had in God, and which served only to increase my faith), I found myself changed all at once.

My soul, which until that time was in trouble, felt a profound inward peace,[8] as if it were in its center and place of rest.

Ever since that time I have walked before God, simply, in faith, with humility,[9] and with love,[10] and I apply myself diligently to do nothing and think nothing that may displease Him.

I hope that when I have done what I can, He will do with me what He pleases.

As for what occurs in me at present, I cannot express it. I have no pain or difficulty about my state, because I have no will but that of God, which I endeavor to accomplish in all things. I am so resigned to His will that I would not take up a straw from the ground against His order, or from any other motive than purely that of love for Him.[11]

I have stopped all forms of devotion and set prayers but those to which my state[12] obliges me. I make it my business only to persevere in His holy presence, wherein I keep myself by a simple attention and a general fond regard for God, which I may call an actual presence of God. Or, to speak better, an habitual, silent, and secret communion of the soul with God, which often causes me joys and raptures inwardly, and sometimes also outwardly, so great that I am forced to use means to moderate them and prevent their appearance to others.

In short, I am assured beyond all doubt that my soul has been with God above these thirty years. I pass over many things that I may not be tedious to you, yet I think it proper to inform you in what manner I consider myself before God, whom I behold as my King.[13]

I consider myself as the most wretched of men, inwardly full of sores and corruption, and one who has committed all sorts of crimes against his King.

Touched with a sensible[14] regret, I confess to Him all my wickedness, I ask His forgiveness,[15] and I abandon myself into His hands so that He may do what He pleases with me.

But the King, full of mercy and goodness, very far from chastising me, embraces me with love, makes me eat at His table, serves me with His own hands, and gives me the key to His treasures.

He converses and delights Himself with me incessantly, in a thousand and a thousand ways, and treats me in all respects as His favorite.

It is in this way that I consider myself from time to time in His holy presence.

My most useful method is this simple attention, and a general passionate regard for God, to whom I find myself often attached with greater sweetness and delight than that of an infant at the mother's breast.

So much so that, if I dare use the expression, I would choose to call this state the bosom of God,16 for the inexpressible sweetness that I taste and experience there.

If sometimes my thoughts wander from it by necessity or infirmity, I am presently recalled by inward motions so charming and delicious that I am ashamed to mention them.

I desire your reverence to reflect rather upon my great wretchedness, of which you are fully informed, than upon the great favors that God does for me, all unworthy and ungrateful as I am.

As for my set hours of prayer, they are only a continuation of the same exercise. Sometimes I consider myself there as a stone before a carver, whereof He is to make a statue.

Presenting myself thus before God, I desire Him to form His perfect image in my soul, and make me entirely like Him.

At other times, when I apply myself to prayer, I feel all my spirit and all my soul lift itself up without any care or effort of mine, and it continues as if it were suspended and firmly fixed in God, as in its center and place of rest.

I know that some charge this state with inactivity, delusion, and self-love. I confess that it is a holy inactivity, and would be a happy self-love if the soul in that state were capable of it.

Because, in effect, while it is in this repose it cannot be disturbed by such acts as it was formerly accustomed to, and which were then it's support, but which would now rather hinder than assist it.

Yet I cannot bear that this should be called delusion, because the soul that in this manner enjoys God desires nothing but Him.

If this be delusion in me, it belongs to God to remedy it.

Let Him do what He pleases with me.

I desire only Him, and to be wholly devoted to Him.

You will, however, oblige me in sending me your opinion, to which I always pay a great deference, for I have great esteem for your reverence, and am,

In our Lord;

Yours ...

In this letter Brother Lawrence reflects to a spiritual director about the first ten years of his religious life. He wrote this letter 45 years after his entrance into the order in June 1640.

Third Letter

Sometime before November 1685

To My Dearest Prioress,

Today I received two books and a letter from Sister ____, who is preparing to make her profession,[17] and upon that account desires the prayers of your holy society, and yours in particular. I know that she counts much upon them, so please do not disappoint her.

Beseech of God that she may make her sacrifice for His love alone, and make a firm resolution to be wholly devoted to Him.

I will send you one of these books that treat of the presence of God.

This is a subject that, in my opinion, contains the whole spiritual life, and it seems to me that whoever practices it in a proper manner will soon become spiritual.

I know that to practice it right, the heart must be empty of all other things, because God will possess the heart by Himself alone.

He cannot possess it alone without emptying it of everything besides Him, so neither can He act there and do in it what He pleases, unless it is left vacant to Him.[18]

There is not in the world a kind of life more sweet and delightful than that of a continual communion with God. Only those who practice and experience it can comprehend it. Yet I do not advise you to do it for that motive. It is not pleasure that we should seek in this exercise—we should do it from a principle of love, and because God would have us do it.

If I were a preacher, I would above all other things preach the practice of the presence of God. If I were a director,19 I would advise all the world to do it, so necessary do I think it is, and so easy, too.

Ah! if we but knew the lack we have of the grace and assistance of God, we would never lose sight of Him—not for a moment. Believe me, and make immediately a holy and firm resolution never to forget Him willfully. Resolve also to spend the rest of your days in His sacred presence, deprived of all consolations for the love of Him, if He so thinks fit.

Set heartily about this work, and if you do it as you should, be assured that you well know the effects of it. I will assist you with my prayers, poor as they are.

I recommend myself earnestly to your prayers and those of your holy society, being theirs, and more particularly;

Yours ...

Fourth Letter

November 3, 1685

Dearest Prioress,

I have received from Mrs. ___ the things that you gave her for me. I wonder that you have not given me your thoughts about the little book I sent to you, and which you must have received. Do set heartily about the practice of it in your old age—it is better late than never.

I cannot imagine how religious people can live satisfied without the practice of the presence of God. For my part, I keep myself secluded with Him in the source or center of my soul as much as I can. While I am thus with Him I fear nothing, but the least turning from Him is intolerable. This exercise does not fatigue the body very much.

It is, however, proper to deprive it sometimes—no, often—of many little pleasures that are innocent and lawful. For God will not permit the soul that desires to be devoted entirely to Him to have pleasures other than those with Him—that is more than reasonable.

I do not say that we must, therefore, put violent constraint upon ourselves. No, we must serve God in a holy freedom. We must do our business faithfully, without being troubled or uneasy, recalling our mind to God mildly and with tranquility as often as we find it wandering from Him.

It is, however, necessary to put our whole trust in God, laying aside all other cares.[20] At times we must also lay aside certain forms of devotion, which though very good in themselves, are ones that we often continue to engage in unreasonably, for these devotions were only intended as a means to attain to the end.

So when by this exercise of the presence of God we are with Him who is our end, it is then useless to return to the means that we used to arrive at this state. But we may continue with Him our communion of love, persevering in His holy presence. We do this by an act of praise, of adoration, or of desire. Or by an act of resignation or thanksgiving. And in all the ways that our spirit can invent.

Be not discouraged by the repugnance that you may find in it from nature—you must do yourself violence. At first you may often think it is lost time, but you must go on and resolve to persevere in it to [the day of your] death, in spite of all the difficulties that may occur.

I recommend myself to the prayers of your holy society, and to yours in particular.

I am, in our Lord,

Yours ...

Fifth Letter

Dear Madame,

Though of little worth, my prayers are with you as I promised. I will keep my word. How happy we would be if we could only find the treasure of which the gospel speaks. Nothing else would matter. Since it is inexhaustible, the more we search the more riches we find. Let us devote ourselves ceaselessly to looking for it. Let us not grow weary[21] until we have found it.[22]

Finally, I do not know what will become of me. It seems to me that peace of mind and soul comes to me in my sleep. I only know that God looks after me. My tranquility is so great that I fear nothing.[23] What could I fear when I am with Him?[24] I cling to Him with all my strength.

May He be blessed by all, Amen.

Yours ...

This lady belonged to the religious order.

Sixth Letter

October 12, 1688

My Dearest Lady,

We have a God who is infinitely gracious and knows all about our needs.[25] I always thought that He would reduce you to the greatest degree. He will come in His own time, and when you least expect it. Hope in Him more than ever. Thank Him with me for the favors He does for you, particularly for the fortitude and patience that He gives you in your afflictions. It is a plain mark of the care He takes of you.

Comfort yourself, therefore, with Him, and give thanks for all.

I admire also the fortitude and bravery of Mr. ___. God has given him a good disposition and a good will, but there is in him still a little of the world and a great deal of youth. I hope the affliction that God has sent him will prove a wholesome remedy to him, and make him enter into himself. It is an accident that should engage him to put all his trust in Him who accompanies him everywhere. Let him think of Him as often as he can, especially in the greatest dangers.

A little lifting up of the heart is enough. A little remembrance of God, one act of inward worship, though upon a march and with a sword in hand, are prayers that, however short, are nevertheless very acceptable to God. Far from lessening a soldier's courage in occasions of danger, they best serve to fortify it. Let him, therefore, think of God as much as he can.

Let him accustom himself, by degrees, to this small but holy exercise. No one will notice it, and nothing is easier than to repeat often in the day these little internal adorations. Recommend to him, if you please, that he think of God as much as he can, in the manner here directed.

It is very fit and most necessary for a soldier who is daily exposed to the dangers of life.

I hope that God will assist him and all the family, to whom I present my service, being theirs and,

Yours ...

Seventh Letter

Dear Madame,

You tell me nothing new, for you are not the only one that is troubled with wandering thoughts. Our mind is extremely roving, but as the will is ruler of all our faculties, it must recall them and carry them to God as their last end.

When the mind isn't adequately disciplined when we first become engaged in devotion, it often develops certain bad habits of wandering and amusing itself. These habits are difficult to overcome and commonly draw us to the things of the earth, even against our wills.

I believe one remedy for this is to confess our faults and to humble ourselves before God.[26] I do not advise you to use a lot of words in prayer, for many words and long discourses are often the reason our mind wanders. Hold yourself in prayer before God like a dumb or paralytic beggar at a rich man's gate. Let it be your business to keep your mind in the presence of the Lord.

If your mind sometimes wanders and withdraws itself from Him, do not upset yourself about it. Troubled thoughts and uneasiness serve to distract the mind rather than to recall it—the will must bring it back into tranquility. If you persevere in this manner, God will have pity on you.

One way to recall the mind easily in the time of prayer, and preserve it more in tranquility, is not to let it wander too far at other times. You should keep it strictly in the presence of God. Being accustomed to think of Him often, you will find it easy to keep your mind calm in the time of prayer, or at least to recall it from its wanderings.[27]

I have told you already in general, in my former letters, of the advantages we may draw from this practice of the presence of God.

Let us set about it seriously, and pray for one another.

Yours ...

The recipient of this letter was probably a former Prioress.

Eighth Letter

March 28, 1689

Dearest Prioress,

The enclosed is an answer to the letter that I received from ___, please deliver it to her. She seems to me full of good will, but she wants to go faster than grace. One does not become holy all at once. I recommend her to you—we should help one another by our advice, and yet more by our good examples. You will oblige me by letting me hear about her from time to time, and whether she is very fervent and very obedient.

Let us think often, therefore, that our only business in this life is to please God, and that anything besides that is foolishness and vanity.

You and I have lived about forty years in religion (i.e., a monastic life). Have we employed them in loving and serving God, who by His mercy has called us to this state, and for that very end? I am filled with shame and confusion when I reflect on one hand upon the great favors that God has done and insistently continues to do for me, and on the other upon the ill use I have made of them and my small advancement in the way of perfection.

Since by His mercy He gives us still a little time, let us begin in earnest. Let us repair the lost time. Let us return with a full assurance to that Father of mercies, who is always ready to receive us affectionately. Let us renounce, let us generously renounce, for the love of Him, all that is not Him. He deserves infinitely more. Let us think of Him perpetually. Let us put all our trust in Him. I do not doubt but we will soon realize the effects of it in receiving the abundance of His grace, with which we can do all things, and without which we can do nothing but sin.

We cannot escape the dangers that abound in life without the actual and continual help of God. Let us, therefore, pray to Him for it continually. How can we pray to Him without being with Him? How can we be with Him except by thinking of Him often?

And how can we often think of Him except by making a holy habit of it? You will tell me that I am always saying the same thing. It is true, for this is the best and easiest method I know. And since I use no other, I advise all the world to do it. We must know God before we can love Him. To know God, we must often think of Him.

And when we come to love Him, we will think of Him often, for our heart will be with our treasure. This is an argument that well deserves your consideration.

I am,

Yours ...

Ninth Letter

Dearest Lady,

I pity you very much.

It will be of great importance if you can leave the care of your affairs to _____, and spend the remainder of your life only in worshiping God.

God requires no great matters of us:

A little remembrance of Him from time to time.

A little adoration.

Sometimes to pray for His grace.

Sometimes to offer Him your sufferings.

Sometimes to return Him thanks for the favors He has given you (and still gives you, in the midst of your troubles).

To console yourself with Him as often as you can.

Lift up your heart to Him, sometimes even at your meals, and when you are in company. The least little remembrance will always be acceptable to Him. You need not cry very loud, for He is nearer to us than we are aware of.

It is not necessary to always be at church to be with God. We may make our heart a prayer chapel that we can retire to from time to time to converse with Him in meekness, humility, and love. Everyone is capable of such familiar communion with God, some more, some less.

He knows what we can do, so let us then begin. Perhaps He expects but one generous resolution on our part. Have courage. We have but little time to live (you are near sixty-four, and I am almost eighty). Let us live and die with God. Sufferings will be sweet and pleasant to us while we are with Him. But the greatest pleasures will be a cruel punishment to us without Him.

May He be blessed for all.

Amen.

Accustom yourself by degrees, therefore, to worship Him in this manner, to beseech His grace, to offer Him your heart from time to time in the midst of your business—even every moment, if you can.

Do not always strictly confine yourself to certain rules, or particular forms of devotion, but act with a general confidence in God, with love and humility.

You may be assured of my poor prayers, and that I am their servant, and particularly

Yours in our Lord ...

Probably written around 1689, since Brother Lawrence mentions that he is almost eighty.

Tenth Letter

October 29, 1689

Dearest Lady,

I have had a good deal of difficulty to bring myself to write to Mr. ___, and I do it now purely because you and Madam desire me to. Please write the directions and send them to him. I am very well pleased with the trust that you have in God–I wish that He may increase it in you more and more. We cannot have too much in so good and faithful a Friend, who will never fail us in this world nor in the next.

If Mr. ___ makes to his advantage the loss he has had and puts all his confidence in God, He will soon give him another friend, more powerful and more inclined to serve him. God disposes of hearts as He pleases.

Perhaps Mr. – was too much attached to the one he has lost. We should love our friends, but without encroaching upon the love due to God, which must be the principal [love we possess].

Please remember what I have recommended to you, which is to think often on God, by day and by night in your business and even in your diversions. He is always near you and with you–do not leave Him alone.

You would think it rude to leave a friend alone who came to visit you–so why must God be neglected? Do not forget Him, therefore, but think about Him often, adore Him continually, live and die with Him—this is the glorious work of a Christian. In a word, this is our profession. If we do not know it, we must learn it. I will endeavor to help you with my prayers, and am, in our Lord,

Yours ...

Eleventh Letter

November 17, 1690

My Dear Madame,

I do not pray that you will be delivered from your pains, but I pray God earnestly that He will give you strength and patience to bear them as long as He pleases.[28] Comfort yourself with Him who holds you fastened to the cross. He will loose you when He thinks fit. Happy are those who suffer with Him.

Accustom yourself to suffer in that manner, and seek from Him the strength to endure as much, and as long, as He judges to be necessary for you. The people of the world do not comprehend these truths, nor is it to be wondered at, since they suffer like what they are and not like Christians.

They consider sickness as a pain to nature, and not as a favor from God. Seeing it only in that light, they find nothing in it but grief and distress. But those who consider sickness as coming from the hand of God, as the effect of His mercy and the means that He employs for their salvation,[29] commonly find in it great sweetness and sensible consolation.

I wish you could convince yourself that God is often (in some sense) nearer to us, and more effectually present with us, in sickness than in health. Rely upon no other physician, for it is my apprehension that He reserves your cure to Himself. Put all your trust in Him, therefore, and you will soon realize the effects of it in your recovery, which we often retard by putting greater confidence in physic than in God.[30]

Whatever remedies you make use of, they will succeed only so far as He permits. When pains come from God, He only can cure them. He often sends diseases of the body to cure those of the soul. Comfort yourself with the sovereign Physician of the soul and the body.[31]

Be satisfied with the condition in which God places you–however happy you may think I am, I envy you. Pains and sufferings would be a paradise to me while I suffered with my God, and the greatest pleasures would be hell to me if I relished them without Him. All my consolation would be to suffer something for His sake.

In a little time I must go to God. What comforts me in this life is that I now see Him by faith.[32] I see Him in such a manner as might make me say sometimes, I believe no more, but I see. I feel what faith teaches us, and in that assurance and that practice of faith I will live and die with Him.[33]

Continue always with God, therefore, it is the only support and comfort for your affliction. I will beseech Him to be with you.

Presenting my service, I am,

Yours ...

This letter was written to a dying ex-Prioress.

Twelfth Letter

My Brother,

Since you desire so earnestly that I should explain to you the method by which I arrived at that habitual sense of God's presence, which out of His mercy our Lord has been pleased to grant me, I must tell you that it is with great difficulty that I am prevailed on by your determination.

I do it now only on the condition that you show my letter to no one.[34] If I knew that you would let it be seen, all the desire that I have for your advancement would not be able to make me write this letter. This is the way that I attained to God's presence.

Having found in many books different methods of going to God, and various practices of the spiritual life, I thought they would puzzle me rather than simplify what I sought after, which was nothing but how to become wholly God's. This made me resolve to give the all for the all—my all for God's all.

After having given myself wholly to God, I renounced for the love of Him everything that was not Him, so that He might take away my sin,[35] and I began to live as if there was no one but He and I in the world. Sometimes I considered myself before Him as a poor criminal at the feet of his judge.

At other times, I beheld Him in my heart as my Father, as my God.

I worshiped Him as often as I could, keeping my mind in His holy presence, and recalling my mind as often as I found it had wandered from Him. I found no small effort in this exercise, and yet I continued it in spite of all the difficulties that occurred, without troubling or disquieting myself when my mind wandered involuntarily. I made this my business as much all the day long as at the appointed times of prayer.

For at all times, every hour, every minute, even in the height of my business, I drove away from my mind everything that was capable of interrupting my thoughts of God.

All that has been my common practice ever since I entered into religion. Although I have done it very imperfectly, I have found great advantages in it. These, I well know, are to be imputed to the mere mercy and goodness of God, because we can do nothing without Him,36 and I still less than any.

But when we are faithful to keep ourselves in His holy presence, and set Him always before us, this keeps us from offending Him and doing anything that may displease Him, at least willfully.

It also produces in us a holy freedom and, if I may so speak, a familiarity with God that enables us to ask successfully for the graces we need.

In brief, by often repeating these acts they become habitual, and the presence of God made natural to us.

Please give Him thanks with me for His great goodness toward me, which I can never sufficiently marvel at, and the many favors He has done for so miserable a sinner as I am.

May all things praise Him. Amen.

I am, in our Lord,

Yours . . .

The recipient of this letter was a fellow member of the religious order.

Thirteenth Letter

November 28, 1690

Dear Madame,

If we were well accustomed to the exercise of the presence of God, all bodily diseases would be much alleviated by it. God often permits that we should suffer a little to purify our souls and oblige us to continue with Him.

Take courage, offer Him your pains incessantly, and pray to Him for strength to endure them. Above all, get a habit of entertaining yourself often with God, and forget Him the least you can. Adore Him in your infirmities, offer yourself to Him from time to time, and in the height of your sufferings beseech Him humbly and affectionately (as a child his father) to make you conformable to His holy will. I will endeavor to assist you with my poor prayers.

God has many ways of drawing us to Himself. He sometimes hides Himself from us. But faith alone, which will not fail us in time of need, should be our support and the foundation of our confidence, which must be all in God.

I do not know how God will dispose of me. I am always happy. All the world suffers, and yet I, who deserve the severest discipline, feel joys so continual and so great that I can scarcely contain them.

I would willingly ask God for a part of your sufferings, except that I know my weakness, which is so great that if He left me for one moment to myself I would be the most wretched man alive.

Yet I do not know how He can leave me alone, because faith gives me as strong a conviction as sense can that He never forsakes us until we first forsake Him.[37]

Let us fear to leave Him.

Let us be always with Him.

Let us live and die in His presence.

Pray for me as I do for you.

I am,

Yours ...

This letter was written to the same former prioress that receives letters 14, 15, and 16.

Fourteenth Letter

December 21, 1690

My Dear Madame,

I am in pain to see you suffer so long. What gives me some ease and sweetens the feelings I have for your griefs is that they are proofs of God's love toward you. See them in that view and you will bear them more easily. As your case is, it is my opinion that you should leave off human remedies, and resign yourself entirely to the providence of God. Perhaps He waits only for that resignation and a perfect trust in Him to cure you.[38]

Since, notwithstanding all your cares, physic has hitherto proved unsuccessful, and your ailment still increases, it will not be tempting God to abandon yourself into His hands and expect all from Him.

I told you in my last that He sometimes permits bodily diseases to cure the illnesses of the soul. Have courage, therefore. Make a virtue of necessity.

Do not ask God for deliverance from your pains, but strength to bear them resolutely for the love of Him—all that He pleases [wills or desires] and as long as He pleases.

Such prayers are, indeed, a little hard to nature, but most acceptable to God, and sweet to those that love Him.

Love sweetens pains. When one loves God, one suffers for His sake with joy and courage. Do this I beseech you, and comfort yourself with Him who is the only physician of all our ailments.

He is the Father of the afflicted, always ready to help us. He loves us infinitely more than we imagine. Love Him, therefore, and seek no consolation elsewhere. I hope you will soon receive it.

Adieu.

I will help you with my prayers, poor as they are, and will always be, in our Lord,

Yours ...

Fifteenth Letter

January 22, 1691

My Dear Prioress,

I give thanks to our Lord for having relieved you a little, according to your desire. I have been often near expiring, but I never was so much satisfied as then. Accordingly, I did not pray for any relief, but I prayed for strength to suffer with courage, humility, and love. Ah, how sweet it is to suffer with God! However great the sufferings may be, receive them with love.

It is paradise to suffer and be with Him. If we would enjoy the peace of paradise in this life, we must accustom ourselves to familiar, humble, affectionate communion with Him.

We must not let our spirit wander from Him on any occasion. We must make our heart a spiritual temple in which to adore Him incessantly. We must watch continually over ourselves so that we will not do, say, or think anything that will displease Him. When we occupy our minds with God in this manner, suffering will become full of unction and consolation.

I know that to arrive at this state the beginning is very difficult, for we must act purely in faith. But though it is difficult, we know also that we can do all things with the grace of God, which He never refuses to those who ask for it earnestly.[39]

Knock, persevere in knocking,[40] and I answer for it that He will open to you in His due time, and will grant you all at once what He has deferred for many years.

Adieu.

Pray to Him for me, as I pray to Him for you. I hope to see Him quickly.

I am,

Yours ...

Sixteenth Letter

February 6, 1691

My Madame,

God knows best what is needful for us, and all that He does is for our good. If we knew how much He loves us, we would always be ready to receive equally and with indifference from His hand the sweet and the bitter. All would please us that came from Him. Distressful afflictions never appear intolerable, except when we see them in the wrong light.

When we see them as dispensed by the hand of God, when we know that it is our loving Father who humbles and distresses us, our sufferings will lose their bitterness and even become matters of consolation.

Let all our occupation be to know God.[41] The more we know Him, the more we desire to know Him. Since knowledge is commonly the measure of love, the deeper and more extensive our knowledge is, the greater will be our love. If our love of God were great, we would love Him equally in pains and pleasures.

Let us not content ourselves with loving God for the mere sensible favors that He has done or may do for us, no matter how elevated they are. Such favors, though ever so great, cannot bring us as near to Him as faith does in one simple act. Let us seek Him often by faith. He is within us—do not seek Him elsewhere. If we do love Him alone, are we not rude, and do we not deserve blame, if we busy ourselves about trifles that do not please and perhaps offend Him? It is to be feared these trifles will one day cost us dearly.

Let us begin to be devoted to Him in good earnest. Let us cast everything besides Him out of our hearts. He will possess them alone. Beseech this favor of Him. If we do what we can on our parts, we will soon see the change wrought in us that we aspire after. I cannot thank Him sufficiently for the relaxation He has bestowed upon you.

I hope that from His mercy He grants me the favor to see Him within a few days.[42]

Let us pray for one another.

I am, in our Lord,

Yours ...

Endnotes

1 *Prioress*: Nun in charge of a priory; ranking in authority just below an abbess of an abbey.

2 1 John 2:5, 5:3

3 John 3:8

4 Mark 4:39

5 Romans 5:5

6 The following note was written by an editor from many years ago, probably the original compiler of Brother Lawrence's letters. "I suppose he means that all distinct notions he could form of God were unsatisfactory, because he perceived them to be unworthy of God, and therefore his mind was not to be satisfied but by the views of faith. Such views understand God to be infinite and incomprehensible, as He is in Himself, and not as He can be conceived by human ideas."

7 Romans 8:31

8 Philippians 4:7

9 Daniel 10:12; 1 Peter 5:5

10 1 Corinthians 13—For a detailed study on the type of love Paul wrote about in this chapter, read the Pure Gold Classic edition of *The Greatest Thing in the World* by Henry Drummond, published by Bridge-Logos Publishers.

11 Luke 10:27

12 His position in the monastery.

13 1 Timothy 6:15; Revelation 17:14, 19:16

14 *Sensible*: Perceptible by the senses or by the mind.

15 1 John 1:9

16 John 1:18

17 Take her vows as a nun.

18 Revelation 3:20

19 It was the function of the director to give religious counsel in those various circumstances in which Christians, especially in the beginning of their religious life, were found to need it.

20 1 Peter 5:7

21 Galatians 6:9

22 Matthew 13:45-46

23 2 Timothy 1:7

24 Romans 8:31

25 Luke 12:30

26 James 5:16; 1 Peter 5:6

27 2 Timothy 1:7

28 2 Corinthians 12:7-10

29 Ephesians 2:8-9

30 *Physic*: Archaic. The art or profession of medicine. Considering the state of medicine and the sometimes almost barbaric treatment that was given the sick in Brother Lawrence's day, it is easy to understand why he had little confidence in it. But one of the strongest forces that God has placed in us is self-preservation, both of our life and our health. It is inconceivable that God would have done so, and yet not expect us to use all the intellect he has given us, and all that he has placed in the earth, to preserve both.

31 Exodus 15:26

32 Hebrews 11:6

33 Ephesians 3:17

34 Brother Lawrence's letters were not published until after his death.

35 Matthew 1:21

36 John 15:5

37 Deuteronomy 31:6; Hebrews 13:5

38 Psalm 103:2-5

39 Hebrews 4:16

40 Luke 11:9-10

41 Philippians 3:8-11

42 Brother Lawrence took to his bed two days later, and died within six days after writing this letter, on Monday, February 12, 1691, at 9:00 A.M.

V
Ways of Attaining the
Presence of God

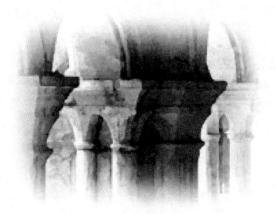

Essential Conditions for Attaining the Presence of God

The first is a great purity of life in which we guard ourselves with extreme care lest we should do, say, or think anything that might be displeasing to God.

When any such thing happens, we need to repent of it immediately and humbly beseech His forgiveness.

The second is a great faithfulness in the practice of His Presence, and in keeping the soul's gaze fixed on God in faith, calmly, humbly, lovingly, without allowing anxious cares and worries to enter in.

Make it your study, before taking up any task, to look to God, if only for a moment. Do this often while you are performing the task, and also when you have finished.

Since this cannot become a habitual practice without time and great patience, do not be disheartened at your many failures.

This habit can only be formed with difficulty, but once it is formed, your joy in it will be great!

The heart is the first thing in us to have life, and it has dominion over all the body.[1]

Therefore it is right that it should be the first and last to love and worship God, both when we begin and end our actions, whether they are spiritual or bodily.

This should generally be the same in all the affairs of life. It is in the heart, therefore, that we should strive to make a habit of gazing on God,[2] until the action that is needed to bring the heart to this obedience is done quite simply and naturally, without strain or study.

To those who set out upon this practice let me suggest a few words, such as "My God, I am wholly Thine," "O God of love, I love Thee with all my heart," "Lord, make my heart even as Thine," or other such words as love prompts at the moment.

But be careful that your mind does not wander back to the world again. Keep it fixed on God alone, so that controlled by your will it shall continue to abide with God.

The practice of the presence of God is somewhat hard in the beginning, yet pursued faithfully it imperceptibly works most marvelous effects within the soul.[3]

It draws down God's grace abundantly, and leads the soul imperceptibly to the ever-present vision of God, loving and beloved.

This is the most spiritual and most real, the most free and most life-giving manner of prayer.

Remember that to attain to this state, we must mortify the senses.[4] No soul that takes delight in earthly things can find full joy in the presence of God.

To be with Him we must leave behind the creature.[5]

Necessary Practices for Attaining the Spiritual Life

The practice that is the most holy, the most general, and the most needful in the spiritual life is the practice of the presence of God.

It is the schooling of the soul to find its joy in His divine companionship.

It is to hold with Him humble and loving communion without set rule or stated method, at all times and at every moment. And to do it during all times of our temptations and tribulations, in all times of our dryness of soul and disrelish of God, and, yes, even when we fall into unfaithfulness and actual sin.

We should apply ourselves unceasingly to so ruling all our actions that they become little acts of communion with God.

But such communion must not be contrived, it must come naturally from the purity and simplicity of the heart.

We must do all things thoughtfully and soberly without being impulsive or impatient, which indicates an undisciplined mind.

We must go about our work quietly, calmly, and lovingly, entreating Him to prosper the works of our hands.

By thus keeping heart and mind fixed on God, we will bruise the head of the evil one and beat his weapons down to the ground.

When we are busy, or meditating on spiritual things, even in our time of set devotion [religious services], while our voice is rising in prayer [or song], we should not cease for one brief moment to worship God in the depth of our being as often as we can—to taste Him [spiritually] though it be in [a] passing [moment], to touch Him as it were by stealth.[7]

Since you must know that God is with you in all you undertake, that He is at the very depth and center of your soul, why should you not pause for an instant from time to time in your outward business, and even in the act of prayer, to worship Him within your soul, to praise Him, to entreat His aid, to offer Him the service of your heart, and give Him thanks for all His loving kindnesses and tender mercies?

What offering is there more acceptable to God than throughout the day to quit the outward things of the senses, and to withdraw within the secret places of the soul to worship Him?

Besides, by so doing we destroy the love of self, which can subsist only among the things of the senses, and which we are rid of during these quiet times with God without being conscious of it.

Truly, we can render no greater or more definite proofs of our trust and faithfulness to God, than by turning from things created to find our joy, even though for a single moment, in our Creator.

But do not think that I am counseling you to disregard completely and forever the outward things that are around us.

Since that is impossible, prudence, the mother of virtues, must be your guide.

Yet, I am confident that it is a common error among religious people to neglect this practice of stopping what they are doing for a while to worship God in the depth of their soul, and to enjoy the peace of brief communion with Him.

Our acts of worship are to be prompted and guided by faith.

We must genuinely believe that God is in very fact within our hearts, and that we must worship Him, love Him, and serve Him in spirit and in truth.[8]

We must further believe that He sees all, and that all hearts are open to Him, our own and those of all His creatures.

Additionally, we must believe that He is self-existent, and that in Him all His creatures live and move and have their being.[9]

We must also believe that His perfection is infinite and sovereign, and demands the full surrender of ourselves, our souls and our bodies.

In simple justice we owe Him all our thoughts, words, and actions. Let us see to it that we pay our debt.

Necessity is laid upon us to examine ourselves with diligence to find out what virtues we chiefly lack, and which are the hardest for us to acquire.

We should seek to learn the sins that most easily beset us,[10] and the times and occasions [in particular] when we most often fail.

In the time of struggle we should have recourse to God with perfect confidence,[11] abiding steadfast in the presence of His divine majesty.

[Standing before Him] in lowly adoration we should tell Him our griefs and our failures, asking Him lovingly for the assistance of His grace.[12]

In our weakness we shall find in Him our strength.[13]

Always Consider the Glory of God

We must always think carefully how to consider God and His Glory in all that we do, and say, and undertake.

This is the goal that we should set before ourselves, to offer to God a sacrifice of perfect worship in this life, as we hope to do through all eternity.

We should firmly resolve to overcome, with the grace of God assisting us, the many difficulties that will meet us in the spiritual life.

When we enter upon the spiritual life, we should consider thoroughly what we are, probing ourselves to the very depth.

[When we do,] we will find that we are altogether deserving of contempt, unworthy of the name of Christ, prone to all manner of unwholesome conditions, and subject to countless infirmities that distress us and impair the soul's health, rendering us wavering and unstable in our humors14 and dispositions.

In fact, we are creatures whom it is God's will to chasten and make humble[15] by numberless afflictions and adversities, internally as well as externally.

We must believe steadfastly, without once doubting, that such discipline is for our good.

It is God's will to visit us with chastening,[16] and is the course of His divine providence to permit our souls to pass through all manner of sore experiences and times of trial.

For the love of God, we should undergo various sorrows and afflictions [without complaining] for so long as seems needful to Him. Without this submission of heart and spirit to the will of God, devotion and perfection cannot exist or continue.

The higher a soul aspires to perfection, the more dependent it is on grace.

Also, the grace of God is increasingly needed for each moment [of the soul's development], for without it the soul can do nothing.

The world, the flesh, and the devil join forces and assault the soul so distressfully and untiringly, that without its humble reliance on the ever-present aid of God they would drag it down in spite of all resistance.

To rely that way on God's aid seems hard to nature, but grace makes it become easy, and brings with it joy.

We Are Required to Worship God in Spirit and in Truth

There are three points in the above statement that must be explained:

1. To worship God in spirit and in truth means to offer to Him the worship that we owe.

God is a Spirit, therefore we must worship Him in spirit and in truth. That is to say, by presenting to Him a true and humble spiritual worship in the very depth of our being.

God alone can see this worship, which, offered unceasingly, will in the end become as it were natural, and as if He were one with our soul, and our soul one with Him. Practice will make this clear.

2. To worship God in truth is to acknowledge Him to be what He truly is, and ourselves as what we truly are.

To worship Him in truth is to acknowledge with heart-felt sincerity what God truly is—that is, to say, infinitely perfect, worthy of infinite adoration, infinitely removed from sin, and equally so of all His divine attributes.

[It is also to recognize] that those are little guided by reason who do not employ all their powers to render to this great God the worship that is His due.

3. Furthermore, to worship God in truth is to confess that we live our lives entirely contrary to His will.

We also live contrary to our knowledge that if we were just willing, He would willingly make us conformable to Him.

Who will be guilty of the folly of withholding even for a moment the reverence and the love, the service and the unceasing worship, that we owe to Him?

Union of the Soul with God

There are three degrees of union of the soul with God. The first degree is general, the second is virtual union, and the third is actual union.

1. The degree of union is general when the soul is united to God solely by grace.

2. Virtual union (which is in effect union, though not in fact) is when we are united to God at the beginning of an action, and remain united to Him by reason of that action for only such time as it lasts.

3. Actual union is the perfect union. In the other degrees the soul is passive, almost as it were slumbering. In this actual union the soul is intensely active—quicker than fire are its operations, more luminous than the sun, unobstructed by any passing cloud.

Yet we can be deceived as to this union by our feelings. This union is not a mere fleeting emotion, such as would prompt a passing cry like, "My God, I love Thee with my heart's full strength."

It is, instead, a state of soul—if I can but find words—that is deeply spiritual and yet very simple, which fills us with a joy that is undisturbed, and with a love that is very humble and very reverent.

It is a union that lifts the soul aloft to heights where the sense of the love of God compels it to adore Him, and to embrace Him with a tenderness that cannot be expressed, and which experience alone can teach us to understand.

All who aspire to union with the Divine should know [be warned] that whatever [earthly thing] can gladden the will is in fact pleasing [and attractive] to it, or at least so the will considers it.

There is no one but must acknowledge that God is beyond our understanding. To be united to Him it is necessary, therefore, to deny the will all [earthly] tastes and pleasures, bodily and spiritual, so that, being thus detached, it can be free to love God above all things.

For if the will can in any measure come to know God, it can do so only through love. The difference is great between the tastes and sentiments of the will and its working. The limits of the will's tastes and sentiments are in the soul. But its working, which is properly love, finds its only limit in God.

The Presence of God

The presence of God is an application of our spirit to God, or a realization of God as present, which is borne home to us either by the imagination or by the understanding.

I have a friend who these forty years past has been practicing through his understanding a realization of the presence of God.

To it he gives many other names—sometimes he calls it a simple act, or a clear and distinct knowledge of God.

At other times, he refers to it as a view as through a glass, a loving gaze, an inward sense of God.

Yet again, he terms it a waiting on God, a silent communicating with Him, a repose in Him, the life and peace of the soul.

Still, my friend tells me that all these ways in which he has expressed his sense of the presence of God, come to the same thing.

My friend further states that the presence now fills his soul quite naturally, and that the naturalness came to pass in the following way.

By non-wearying efforts, by constantly recalling his mind to the presence of God, a habit has formed within him of such a nature that as soon as he is freed from his ordinary labor, and often even when he is engaged in his work, his soul lifts itself above all earthly matters, without deliberation or forethought on his part, and fixes itself firmly upon God as its center and place of rest.

At such times, there almost always comes to him a great sense of faith in God.

It is then his soul's joy is full—what he calls the actual presence of God, and includes all other kinds [of joy or of the presence of God] and much more besides.

In that state he feels that only God and he are in the world—holding with Him unbroken communion, asking from Him the supply of all his needs, and finding in His presence fullness of joy.

Let us note well, however, that he holds this communion with God in the depth of his being.

It is there that the soul speaks to God, heart to heart, and throughout the soul who is so communicating there is infused a great and profound peace.

All that occurs externally concerns such a soul no more than a fire of straw, which the more it flares the sooner it burns itself out.

And rarely indeed do the cares of this world intrude to trouble the peace that is within.

But to come back to our consideration of the presence of God.

You must know that the tender and loving light of God's countenance kindles imperceptibly within the soul that ardently embraces it, a fire of love to God that is so great and so divine that it is necessary for the person who is so affected to moderate the outward expression of their feelings.

Great would be our surprise, if we but knew what communion the soul holds at these times with God.

He seems to so delight in this communion, that to the soul who would willingly abide forever with Him, He bestows favors past numbering.

It is as if He was so concerned that the soul would turn again to things of earth, that He provides for it abundantly so that it finds in faith divine nourishment and immeasurable joy that is far beyond its utmost thought and desire—and all without a single effort on its part but simple consent.

The presence of God is thus the life and nourishment of the soul.

Benefits of the Presence of God

The first benefit that the soul receives from the presence of God is that faith becomes more alive and active in all the events of life, particularly when we feel our need, since it obtains for us the assistance of His grace when we are tempted and in every time of trial.

Having learned by this practice to take faith as a guide, the soul, by simply remembering past occurrences, sees and feels God present, and calls upon Him freely and with assurance of an answer, thus receiving the supply of all its needs.

By faith, it would seem, the soul draws very near to the state of the Blessed.

The higher it advances, the more alive faith becomes, until at last the eye of faith is so piercing that the soul can almost say, "Faith is swallowed up in sight"—I see and I experience.[17]

The practice of the presence of God strengthens us in hope. Our hope grows in proportion as our knowledge grows, and in measure as our faith—by this holy practice—penetrates into the hidden mysteries of God.

In like measure it finds in Him a beauty beyond comparison, surpassing infinitely that of earth, and that of the most holy souls [in heaven] and angels.

Our hope grows and becomes ever stronger, sustained and encouraged by the fullness of the bliss [it sees in faith] that it has as its goal, and which it already partially tastes.

Hope breathes into the will a distrust of things seen, and sets it aflame with the consuming fire of God's love. For God's love is truly a consuming fire, burning to ashes all that is contrary to His will.

The soul that is thus kindled cannot live except in the presence of God.

This presence also works within the heart a consecrated zeal, a holy ardor, a violent passion to see this God become known and loved and served and worshiped by all His creatures.

By the practice of the presence of God, by a steadfast gaze upon Him, the soul comes to a knowledge of God that is full and deep—as to an unclouded vision.

Ever after its life is passed in unceasing acts of love and worship, of contrition and of simple trust, of praise and prayer, and service.

At times, life indeed seems to be but one long unbroken practice of His divine presence.

I know that there are not many who reach this state. It is a grace that God bestows only on very few chosen souls, for this unclouded vision is a gift from His bountiful hand.

Yet, for the consolation of those who would willingly embrace this holy practice, let me say that God seldom denies this gift to those who earnestly desire it.

If He does withhold this crowning mercy, be well assured that by the practice of the presence of God and the aid of

His all-sufficient grace, your soul can arrive at a state that approaches very nearly the unclouded vision.

Endnotes

1 Mark 7:21-23

2 Ephesians 3:17

3 Luke 17:20-21

4 *Mortify*: To practice ascetic discipline or self-denial of the body and its appetites.

5 By this, Brother Lawrence undoubtedly means leaving behind those earthly things that delight our human or creature senses.

6 Genesis 3:15

7 Matthew 9:20-21; Mark 5:27-28; Luke 8:44

8 John 4:23-24

9 Acts 17:28

10 Hebrews 12:1

11 Hebrews 4:14-16; 1 John 15:14

12 Hebrews 4:16

13 Philippians 4:13

14 Brother Lawrence is probably referring to the four fluids of the body—blood, phlegm, choler, and black bile, whose relative proportions were thought in ancient physiology to determine a person's disposition and general health.

15 James 4:6, 10; 1 Peter 5:5-6

16 Hebrews 12:5-6

17 Matthew 17:20; Mark 9:23, 11:23-24

VI
Scriptures Relating to the Presence of God

Appendix

Presence of God King James Version
(Manifested Presence and Felt Presence)

Genesis 3:8 And they heard the voice of the LORD God walking in the garden in the cool of the day: and Adam and his wife hid themselves from the presence of the LORD God amongst the trees of the garden.

Genesis 4:14 Behold, thou hast driven me out this day from the face of the earth; and from thy face shall I be hid; and I shall be a fugitive and a vagabond in the earth; and it shall come to pass, that every one that findeth me shall slay me.

Genesis 4:16 And Cain went out from the presence of the LORD, and dwelt in the land of Nod, on the east of Eden.

Genesis 27:7 Bring me venison, and make me savoury meat, that I may eat, and bless thee before the LORD before my death.

Exodus 3:1 Now Moses kept the flock of Jethro his father in law, the priest of Midian: and he led the flock to the backside of the desert, and came to the mountain of God, even to Horeb.

2 And the angel of the LORD appeared unto him in a flame of fire out of the midst of a bush: and he looked, and, behold, the bush burned with fire, and the bush was not consumed.

3 And Moses said, I will now turn aside, and see this great sight, why the bush is not burnt.

4 And when the LORD saw that he turned aside to see, God called unto him out of the midst of the bush, and said, Moses, Moses. And he said, Here am I.

5 And he said, Draw not nigh hither: put off thy shoes from off thy feet, for the place whereon thou standest is holy ground.

Exodus 18:12 And Jethro, Moses' father in law, took a burnt offering and sacrifices for God: and Aaron came, and all the elders of Israel, to eat bread with Moses' father in law before God.

Exodus 19:16 And it came to pass on the third day in the morning, that there were thunders and lightnings, and a thick cloud upon the mount, and the voice of the trumpet exceeding loud; so that all the people that was in the camp trembled.

17 And Moses brought forth the people out of the camp to meet with God; and they stood at the nether part of the mount.

18 And mount Sinai was altogether on a smoke, because the LORD descended upon it in fire: and the smoke thereof ascended as the smoke of a furnace, and the whole mount quaked greatly.

19 And when the voice of the trumpet sounded long, and waxed louder and louder, Moses spake, and God answered him by a voice.

20 And the LORD came down upon mount Sinai, on the top of the mount: and the LORD called Moses up to the top of the mount; and Moses went up.

21 And the LORD said unto Moses, Go down, charge the people, lest they break through unto the LORD to gaze, and many of them perish.

Exodus 25:30 And thou shalt set upon the table showbread before me alway.

Exodus 28:30 And thou shalt put in the breastplate of judgment the Urim and the Thummim; and they shall be upon Aaron's heart, when he goeth in before the LORD: and Aaron shall bear the judgment of the children of Israel upon his heart before the LORD continually.

Exodus 29:11 And thou shalt kill the bullock before the LORD, by the door of the tabernacle of the congregation.

Exodus 33:14 And he said, My presence shall go with thee, and I will give thee rest.

15 And he said unto him, If thy presence go not with me, carry us not up hence.

16 For wherein shall it be known here that I and thy people have found grace in thy sight? is it not in that thou goest with us? so shall we be separated, I and thy people, from all the people that are upon the face of the earth.

Exodus 34:34 But when Moses went in before the LORD to speak with him, he took the veil off, until he came out. And he came out, and spake unto the children of Israel that which he was commanded.

35 And the children of Israel saw the face of Moses, that the skin of Moses' face shone: and Moses put the veil upon his face again, until he went in to speak with him.

Exodus 35:13 The table, and his staves, and all his vessels, and the showbread ...

Exodus 39:36 The table, and all the vessels thereof, and the showbread ...

Leviticus 9:24 And there came a fire out from before the LORD, and consumed upon the altar the burnt offering and the fat: which when all the people saw, they shouted, and fell on their faces.

Leviticus 10:2 And there went out fire from the LORD, and devoured them, and they died before the LORD.

Leviticus 22:3 Say unto them, Whosoever he be of all your seed among your generations, that goeth unto the holy things, which the children of Israel hallow unto the LORD, having his uncleanness upon him, that soul shall be cut off from my presence: I am the LORD.

Numbers 4:7 And upon the table of showbread they shall spread a cloth of blue, and put thereon the dishes, and the spoons, and the bowls, and covers to cover withal: and the continual bread shall be thereon:

Numbers 17:9 Then Moses brought out all the staffs from the Lord's presence to all the Israelites. They looked at them, and each man took his own staff.

Numbers 20:9 So Moses took the staff from the Lord's presence, just as he commanded him.

Deuteronomy 4:37 And because he loved thy fathers, therefore he chose their seed after them, and brought thee out in his sight with his mighty power out of Egypt;

38 To drive out nations from before thee greater and mightier than thou art, to bring thee in, to give thee their land for an inheritance, as it is this day.

Deuteronomy 12:7 And there ye shall eat before the LORD your God, and ye shall rejoice in all that ye put your hand unto, ye and your households, wherein the LORD thy God hath blessed thee.

Deuteronomy 12:18 But thou must eat them before the LORD thy God in the place which the LORD thy God shall choose, thou, and thy son, and thy daughter, and thy manservant, and thy maidservant, and the Levite that is within thy gates: and thou shalt rejoice before the LORD thy God in all that thou puttest thine hands unto.

Deuteronomy 14:23 And thou shalt eat before the LORD thy God, in the place which he shall choose to place his name there, the tithe of thy corn, of thy wine, and of thine oil, and the firstlings of thy herds and of thy flocks; that thou mayest learn to fear the LORD thy God always.

Deuteronomy 14:26 And thou shalt bestow that money for whatsoever thy soul lusteth after, for oxen, or for sheep, or for wine, or for strong drink, or for whatsoever thy soul desireth: and thou shalt eat there before the LORD thy God, and thou shalt rejoice, thou, and thine household ...

Deuteronomy 15:20 Thou shalt eat it before the LORD thy God year by year in the place which the LORD shall choose, thou and thy household.

Deuteronomy 18:6 And if a Levite come from any of thy gates out of all Israel, where he sojourned, and come with all the desire of his mind unto the place which the LORD shall choose;
   7 Then he shall minister in the name of the LORD his God, as all his brethren the Levites do, which stand there before the LORD.

Deuteronomy 19:16 If a false witness rise up against any man to testify against him that which is wrong;
   17 Then both the men, between whom the controversy is, shall stand before the LORD, before the priests and the judges, which shall be in those days ...

Deuteronomy 27:7 And thou shalt offer peace offerings, and shalt eat there, and rejoice before the LORD thy God.

Deuteronomy 29:10 Ye stand this day all of you before the LORD your God; your captains of your tribes, your elders, and your officers, with all the men of Israel,

11 Your little ones, your wives, and thy stranger that is in thy camp, from the hewer of thy wood unto the drawer of thy water:

12 That thou shouldest enter into covenant with the LORD thy God, and into his oath, which the LORD thy God maketh with thee this day:

13 That he may establish thee to day for a people unto himself, and that he may be unto thee a God, as he hath said unto thee, and as he hath sworn unto thy fathers, to Abraham, to Isaac, and to Jacob.

14 Neither with you only do I make this covenant and this oath;

15 But with him that standeth here with us this day before the LORD our God, and also with him that is not here with us this day ...

Joshua 18:6 Ye shall therefore describe the land into seven parts, and bring the description hither to me, that I may cast lots for you here before the LORD our God.

Joshua 18:8 And the men arose, and went away: and Joshua charged them that went to describe the land, saying, Go and walk through the land, and describe it, and come again to me, that I may here cast lots for you before the LORD in Shiloh.

9 And the men went and passed through the land, and described it by cities into seven parts in a book, and came again to Joshua to the host at Shiloh.

10 And Joshua cast lots for them in Shiloh before the LORD: and there Joshua divided the land unto the children of Israel according to their divisions.

Joshua 19:51 These are the inheritances, which Eleazar the priest, and Joshua the son of Nun, and the heads of the fathers of the tribes of the children of Israel, divided for an inheritance by lot in Shiloh before the LORD, at the door of the tabernacle of the congregation. So they made an end of dividing the country.

Judges 18:6 And the priest said to them, "Go in peace. The presence of the LORD be with you on your way" (NKJV).

1 Samuel 2:21 And the LORD visited Hannah, so that she conceived, and bare three sons and two daughters. And the child Samuel grew before the LORD.

1 Samuel 6:19 And he smote the men of Bethshemesh, because they had looked into the ark of the LORD, even he smote of the people fifty thousand and threescore and ten men: and the people lamented, because the LORD had smitten many of the people with a great slaughter.

20 And the men of Bethshemesh said, Who is able to stand before this holy LORD God? and to whom shall he go up from us?

1 Samuel 11:15 And all the people went to Gilgal; and there they made Saul king before the LORD in Gilgal; and there they sacrificed sacrifices of peace offerings before the LORD; and there Saul and all the men of Israel rejoiced greatly.

1 Samuel 12:3 Here I stand. Testify against me in the presence of the LORD and his anointed. Whose ox have I taken? Whose donkey have I taken? Whom have I cheated? Whom have I oppressed? From whose hand have I accepted a bribe to make me shut my eyes? If I have done any of these, I will make it right."

1 Samuel 21:6 So the priest gave him hallowed bread: for there was no bread there but the showbread, that was taken from before the LORD, to put hot bread in the day when it was taken away.

1 Samuel 26:20 Now therefore, let not my blood fall to the earth before the face of the LORD: for the king of Israel is come out to seek a flea, as when one doth hunt a partridge in the mountains.

2 Samuel 22:13 Through the brightness before him were coals of fire kindled.

1 Kings 7:48 And Solomon made all the vessels that pertained unto the house of the LORD: the altar of gold, and the table of gold, whereupon the showbread was ...

1 Kings 8:10 And it came to pass, when the priests were come out of the holy place, that the cloud filled the house of the LORD,

11 So that the priests could not stand to minister because of the cloud: for the glory of the LORD had filled the house of the LORD.

1 Kings 8:28 Yet have thou respect unto the prayer of thy servant, and to his supplication, O LORD my God, to hearken unto the cry and to the prayer, which thy servant prayeth before thee to day ...

1 Kings 17:1 And Elijah the Tishbite, who was of the inhabitants of Gilead, said unto Ahab, As the LORD God of Israel liveth, before whom I stand, there shall not be dew nor rain these years, but according to my word.

1 Kings 19:11 And he said, Go forth, and stand upon the mount before the LORD. And, behold, the LORD passed by, and a great and strong wind rent the mountains, and brake in pieces the rocks before the LORD; but the LORD was not in the wind: and after the wind an earthquake; but the LORD was not in the earthquake:

12 And after the earthquake a fire; but the LORD was not in the fire: and after the fire a still small voice.

13 And it was so, when Elijah heard it that he wrapped his face in his mantle, and went out, and stood in the entering in of the cave. And, behold, there came a voice unto him, and said, What doest thou here, Elijah?

2 Kings 13:23 And the LORD was gracious unto them, and had compassion on them, and had respect unto them, because of his covenant with Abraham, Isaac, and Jacob, and would not destroy them, neither cast he them from his presence as yet.

2 Kings 17:18 Therefore the LORD was very angry with Israel, and removed them out of his sight: there was none left but the tribe of Judah only.

19 Also Judah kept not the commandments of the LORD their God, but walked in the statutes of Israel which they made.

20 And the LORD rejected all the seed of Israel, and afflicted them, and delivered them into the hand of spoilers, until he had cast them out of his sight.

2 Kings 17:22 For the children of Israel walked in all the sins of Jeroboam which he did; they departed not from them;

23 Until the LORD removed Israel out of his sight, as he had said by all his servants the prophets. So was Israel carried away out of their own land to Assyria unto this day.

2 Kings 22:19 Because thine heart was tender, and thou hast humbled thyself before the LORD, when thou heardest what I spake against this place, and against the inhabitants thereof, that they should become a desolation and a curse, and hast rent thy clothes, and wept before me; I also have heard thee, saith the LORD.

2 Kings 23:3 And the king stood by a pillar, and made a covenant before the LORD, to walk after the LORD, and to keep his commandments and his testimonies and his statutes with all their heart and all their soul, to perform the words of this covenant that were written in this book. And all the people stood to the covenant.

2 Kings 23:27 And the LORD said, I will remove Judah also out of my sight, as I have removed Israel, and will cast off this city Jerusalem which I have chosen, and the house of which I said, My name shall be there.

2 Kings 24:3 Surely these things happened to Judah according to the Lord's command, in order to remove them from his presence because of the sins of Manasseh and all he had done,

4 including the shedding of innocent blood. For he had filled Jerusalem with innocent blood, and the LORD was not willing to forgive.

2 Kings 24:20 For through the anger of the LORD it came to pass in Jerusalem and Judah, until he had cast them out from his presence, that Zedekiah rebelled against the king of Babylon.

1 Chronicles 29:22 And did eat and drink before the LORD on that day with great gladness. And they made Solomon the son of David king the second time, and anointed him unto the LORD to be the chief governor, and Zadok to be priest.

2 Chronicles 4:19 And Solomon made all the vessels that were for the house of God, the golden altar also, and the tables whereon the showbread was set ...

2 Chronicles 6:19 Have respect therefore to the prayer of thy servant, and to his supplication, O LORD my God, to hearken unto the cry and the prayer which thy servant prayeth before thee ...

2 Chronicles 20:9 If, when evil cometh upon us, as the sword, judgment, or pestilence, or famine, we stand before this house, and in thy presence, (for thy name is in this house,) and cry unto thee in our affliction, then thou wilt hear and help.

2 Chronicles 34:27 Because thine heart was tender, and thou didst humble thyself before God, when thou heardest his words against this place, and against the inhabitants thereof, and humbledst thyself before me, and didst rend thy clothes, and weep before me; I have even heard thee also, saith the LORD.

2 Chronicles 34:31 And the king stood in his place, and made a covenant before the LORD, to walk after the LORD, and to keep his commandments, and his testimonies, and his statutes, with all his heart, and with all his soul, to perform the words of the covenant which are written in this book.

Ezra 9:15 O LORD God of Israel, thou art righteous: for we remain yet escaped, as it is this day: behold, we are before thee in our trespasses: for we cannot stand before thee because of this.

Job 1:6 Now there was a day when the sons of God came to present themselves before the LORD, and Satan came also among them.

Job 1:12 And the LORD said unto Satan, Behold, all that he hath is in thy power; only upon himself put not forth thine hand. So Satan went forth from the presence of the LORD.

Job 2:1 Again there was a day when the sons of God came to present themselves before the LORD, and Satan came also among them to present himself before the LORD.

Job 2:7 So went Satan forth from the presence of the LORD, and smote Job with sore boils from the sole of his foot unto his crown.

Job 23:15 Therefore am I troubled at his presence: when I consider, I am afraid of him.

Psalm 5:4 For thou art not a God that hath pleasure in wickedness: neither shall evil dwell with thee.

5 The foolish shall not stand in thy sight: thou hatest all workers of iniquity.

Psalm 9:3 When mine enemies are turned back, they shall fall and perish at thy presence.

Psalm 9:19 Arise, O LORD; let not man prevail: let the heathen be judged in thy sight.

Psalm 16:11 Thou wilt show me the path of life: in thy presence is fulness of joy; at thy right hand there are pleasures for evermore.

Psalm 17:2 Let my sentence come forth from thy presence; let thine eyes behold the things that are equal.

Psalm 18:12 At the brightness that was before him his thick clouds passed, hail stones and coals of fire.

Psalm 21:6 For thou hast made him most blessed for ever: thou hast made him exceeding glad with thy countenance.

Psalm 31:20 Thou shalt hide them in the secret of thy presence from the pride of man: thou shalt keep them secretly in a pavilion from the strife of tongues.

Psalm 41:12 And as for me, thou upholdest me in mine integrity, and settest me before thy face for ever.

Psalm 51:11 Cast me not away from thy presence; and take not thy holy spirit from me.

Psalm 61:7 He shall abide before God for ever: O prepare mercy and truth, which may preserve him.

Psalm 68:2 As smoke is driven away, so drive them away: as wax melteth before the fire, so let the wicked perish at the presence of God.

Psalm 68:8 The earth shook; The heavens also dropped rain at the presence of God; Sinai itself was moved at the presence of God, the God of Israel.

Psalm 76:7 You, Yourself, are to be feared; And who may stand in Your presence When once You are angry? (NKJV).

Psalm 89:15 Blessed is the people that know the joyful sound: they shall walk, O LORD, in the light of thy countenance.

Psalm 90:8 Thou hast set our iniquities before thee, our secret sins in the light of thy countenance.

Psalm 95:2 Let us come before his presence with thanksgiving, and make a joyful noise unto him with psalms.

Psalm 97:5 The hills melted like wax at the presence of the LORD, at the presence of the Lord of the whole earth.
Psalm 100:2 Serve the LORD with gladness: come before his presence with singing.

Psalm 101:7 He that worketh deceit shall not dwell within my house: he that telleth lies shall not tarry in my sight.

Psalm 102:28 The children of thy servants shall continue, and their seed shall be established before thee.

Psalm 114:7 Tremble, thou earth, at the presence of the Lord, at the presence of the God of Jacob;

Psalm 139:7 Whither shall I go from thy spirit? or whither shall I flee from thy presence?

8 If I ascend up into heaven, thou art there: if I make my bed in hell, behold, thou art there.

9 If I take the wings of the morning, and dwell in the uttermost parts of the sea;

10 Even there shall thy hand lead me, and thy right hand shall hold me.

11 If I say, Surely the darkness shall cover me; even the night shall be light about me.

12 Yea, the darkness hideth not from thee; but the night shineth as the day: the darkness and the light are both alike to thee.

Psalm 140:13 Surely the righteous shall give thanks unto thy name: the upright shall dwell in thy presence.

Proverbs 8:30 Then I was by him, as one brought up with him: and I was daily his delight, rejoicing always before him;
31 Rejoicing in the habitable part of his earth; and my delights were with the sons of men.

Isaiah 3:8 For Jerusalem is ruined, and Judah is fallen: because their tongue and their doings are against the LORD, to provoke the eyes of his glory.

Isaiah 19:1 The burden of Egypt. Behold, the LORD rideth upon a swift cloud, and shall come into Egypt: and the idols of Egypt shall be moved at his presence, and the heart of Egypt shall melt in the midst of it.

Isaiah 26:17 Like as a woman with child, that draweth near the time of her delivery, is in pain, and crieth out in her pangs; so have we been in thy sight, O LORD.

Isaiah 63:9 In all their affliction he was afflicted, and the angel of his presence saved them: in his love and in his pity he redeemed them; and he bare them, and carried them all the days of old.

Isaiah 64:1 Oh that thou wouldest rend the heavens, that thou wouldest come down, that the mountains might flow down at thy presence.

2 As when the melting fire burneth, the fire causeth the waters to boil, to make thy name known to thine adversaries, that the nations may tremble at thy presence!

3 When thou didst terrible things which we looked not for, thou camest down, the mountains flowed down at thy presence.

Jeremiah 5:22 Fear ye not me? saith the LORD: will ye not tremble at my presence, which have placed the sand for the bound of the sea by a perpetual decree, that it cannot pass it: and though the waves thereof toss themselves, yet can they not prevail; though they roar, yet can they not pass over it?

Jeremiah 7:15 And I will cast you out of my sight, as I have cast out all your brethren, even the whole seed of Ephraim.

Jeremiah 15:1 Then said the LORD unto me, Though Moses and Samuel stood before me, yet my mind could not be toward this people: cast them out of my sight, and let them go forth.

Jeremiah 23:39 Therefore, behold, I, even I, will utterly forget you, and I will forsake you, and the city that I gave you and your fathers, and cast you out of my presence:

40 And I will bring an everlasting reproach upon you, and a perpetual shame, which shall not be forgotten.

Jeremiah 52:3 For through the anger of the LORD it came to pass in Jerusalem and Judah, till he had cast them out from his presence, that Zedekiah rebelled against the king of Babylon.

Lamentations 2:19 Arise, cry out in the night: in the beginning of the watches pour out thine heart like water before the face of the Lord: lift up thy hands toward him for the life of thy young children, that faint for hunger in the top of every street.

Ezekiel 38:19 For in my jealousy and in the fire of my wrath have I spoken, Surely in that day there shall be a great shaking in the land of Israel;

20 So that the fishes of the sea, and the fowls of the heaven, and the beasts of the field, and all creeping things that creep upon the earth, and all the men that are upon the face of the earth, shall shake at my presence, and the mountains shall be thrown down, and the steep places shall fall, and every wall shall fall to the ground.

Ezekiel 44:2 Then said the LORD unto me; This gate shall be shut, it shall not be opened, and no man shall enter in by it; because the LORD, the God of Israel, hath entered in by it, therefore it shall be shut.

3 It is for the prince; the prince, he shall sit in it to eat bread before the LORD; he shall enter by the way of the porch of that gate, and shall go out by the way of the same.

Ezekiel 46:3 Likewise the people of the land shall worship at the door of this gate before the LORD in the sabbaths and in the new moons.

Daniel 7:13 I saw in the night visions, and, behold, one like the Son of man came with the clouds of heaven, and came to the Ancient of days, and they brought him near before him.

14 And there was given him dominion, and glory, and a kingdom, that all people, nations, and languages, should serve him: his dominion is an everlasting dominion, which shall not pass away, and his kingdom that which shall not be destroyed.

Hosea 6:1 Come, and let us return unto the LORD: for he hath torn, and he will heal us; he hath smitten, and he will bind us up.

2 After two days will he revive us: in the third day he will raise us up, and we shall live in his sight.

Jonah 1:3 But Jonah rose up to flee unto Tarshish from the presence of the LORD, and went down to Joppa; and he found a ship going to Tarshish: so he paid the fare thereof, and went down into it, to go with them unto Tarshish from the presence of the LORD.

Jonah 1:10 Then were the men exceedingly afraid, and said unto him, Why hast thou done this? For the men knew that he fled from the presence of the LORD, because he had told them.

Nahum 1:5 The mountains quake at him, and the hills melt, and the earth is burned at his presence, yea, the world, and all that dwell therein.

Zephaniah 1:7 Hold thy peace at the presence of the Lord GOD: for the day of the LORD is at hand: for the LORD hath prepared a sacrifice, he hath bid his guests.

Haggai 1:12 Then Zerubbabel the son of Shealtiel, and Joshua the son of Jehozadak, the high priest, with all the remnant of the people, obeyed the voice of the LORD their God, and the words of Haggai the prophet, as the LORD their God had sent him; and the people feared the presence of the LORD (NKJV).

Zechariah 6:5 And the angel answered and said unto me, These are the four spirits of the heavens, which go forth from standing before the Lord of all the earth.

Malachi 3:16 Then they that feared the LORD spake often one to another: and the LORD hearkened, and heard it, and a book of remembrance was written before him for them that feared the LORD, and that thought upon his name.

Luke 1:19 And the angel answering said unto him, I am Gabriel, that stand in the presence of God; and am sent to speak unto thee, and to show thee these glad tidings.

John 8:38 I speak that which I have seen with my Father: and ye do that which ye have seen with your father.

John 17:5 And now, O Father, glorify thou me with thine own self with the glory which I had with thee before the world was.

Acts 2:26 "Therefore my heart is glad and my tongue rejoices; my body also will live in hope,

    27 because you will not abandon me to the grave, nor will you let your Holy One see decay.

28 You have made known to me the paths of life; you will fill me with joy in your presence."

Acts 2:28 Thou hast made known to me the ways of life; thou shalt make me full of joy with thy countenance.

Acts 3:19 Repent ye therefore, and be converted, that your sins may be blotted out, when the times of refreshing shall come from the presence of the Lord;

20 And he shall send Jesus Christ, which before was preached unto you:

21 Whom the heaven must receive until the times of restitution of all things, which God hath spoken by the mouth of all his holy prophets since the world began.

Acts 9:3 And as he journeyed, he came near Damascus: and suddenly there shined round about him a light from heaven:

4 And he fell to the earth, and heard a voice saying unto him, Saul, Saul, why persecutest thou me?

5 And he said, Who art thou, Lord? And the Lord said, I am Jesus whom thou persecutest: it is hard for thee to kick against the pricks.

Romans 4:17 ... (as it is written, "I have made you a father of many nations") in the presence of Him whom he believed; God, who gives life to the dead and calls those things which do not exist as though they did ...(NKJV).

1 Corinthians 1:29 That no flesh should glory in his presence.

2 Corinthians 2:10 Now whom you forgive anything, I also forgive. For if indeed I have forgiven anything, I have forgiven that one for your sakes in the presence of Christ,

11 lest Satan should take advantage of us; for we are not ignorant of his devices.

2 Corinthians 4:13 We having the same spirit of faith, according as it is written, I believed, and therefore have I spoken; we also believe, and therefore speak;

14 Knowing that he which raised up the Lord Jesus shall raise up us also by Jesus, and shall present us with you.

1 Thessalonians 2:19 For what is our hope, or joy, or crown of rejoicing? Are not even ye in the presence of our Lord Jesus Christ at his coming?

1 Thessalonians 3:9 For what thanks can we render to God again for you, for all the joy wherewith we joy for your sakes before our God;

10 Night and day praying exceedingly that we might see your face, and might perfect that which is lacking in your faith?

1 Thessalonians 3:13 To the end he may stablish your hearts unblameable in holiness before God, even our Father, at the coming of our Lord Jesus Christ with all his saints.

2 Thessalonians 1:9 Who shall be punished with everlasting destruction from the presence of the Lord, and from the glory of his power;

10 When he shall come to be glorified in his saints, and to be admired in all them that believe (because our testimony among you was believed) in that day.

2 Timothy 4:1 I charge thee therefore before God, and the Lord Jesus Christ, who shall judge the quick and the dead at his appearing and his kingdom;

2 Preach the word; be instant in season, out of season; reprove, rebuke, exhort with all longsuffering and doctrine.

Hebrews 6:19 This hope we have as an anchor of the soul, both sure and steadfast, and which enters the Presence behind the veil,

20 where the forerunner has entered for us, even Jesus, having become High Priest forever according to the order of Melchizedek (NKJV)

Hebrews 9:24 For Christ is not entered into the holy places made with hands, which are the figures of the true; but into heaven itself, now to appear in the presence of God for us:

25 Nor yet that he should offer himself often, as the high priest entereth into the holy place every year with blood of others;

26 For then must he often have suffered since the foundation of the world: but now once in the end of the world hath he appeared to put away sin by the sacrifice of himself.

2 Peter 2:10 But chiefly them that walk after the flesh in the lust of uncleanness, and despise government. Presumptuous are they, selfwilled, they are not afraid to speak evil of dignities.

11 Whereas angels, which are greater in power and might, bring not railing accusation against them before the Lord.

1 John 3:19 And hereby we know that we are of the truth, and shall assure our hearts before him.

20 For if our heart condemn us, God is greater than our heart, and knoweth all things.

Jude 1:24 Now unto him that is able to keep you from falling, and to present you faultless before the presence of his glory with exceeding joy,

25 To the only wise God our Saviour, be glory and majesty, dominion and power, both now and for ever. Amen.

Revelation 1:10 On the Lord's Day I was in the Spirit, and I heard behind me a loud voice like a trumpet,

11 which said: "Write on a scroll what you see and send it to the seven churches: to Ephesus, Smyrna, Pergamum, Thyatira, Sardis, Philadelphia and Laodicea."

12 I turned around to see the voice that was speaking to me. And when I turned I saw seven golden lampstands,

13 and among the lampstands was someone "like a son of man," dressed in a robe reaching down to his feet and with a golden sash around his chest.

14 His head and hair were white like wool, as white as snow, and his eyes were like blazing fire.

15 His feet were like bronze glowing in a furnace, and his voice was like the sound of rushing waters.

16 In his right hand he held seven stars, and out of his mouth came a sharp double-edged sword. His face was like the sun shining in all its brilliance.

17 When I saw him, I fell at his feet as though dead. Then he placed his right hand on me and said: "Do not be afraid. I am the First and the Last.

18 I am the Living One; I was dead, and behold I am alive for ever and ever! And I hold the keys of death and Hades.

Revelation 14:10 The same shall drink of the wine of the wrath of God, which is poured out without mixture into the cup of his indignation; and he shall be tormented with fire and brimstone in the presence of the holy angels, and in the presence of the Lamb:

11 And the smoke of their torment ascendeth up for ever and ever: and they have no rest day nor night, who worship the beast and his image, and whosoever receiveth the mark of his name.

Revelation 20:11 And I saw a great white throne, and him that sat on it, from whose face the earth and the heaven fled away; and there was found no place for them.

Study Guide

Biography of Brother Lawrence

1. Brother Lawrence (Nicholas Herman) joined the Roman Catholic Church in 1629. Which religious order did he join?

2. What were Brother Lawrence's duties when he learned to have a "constant conversation with God"?

3. In what ways can you turn drudgery into devotion, as Brother Lawrence did?

4. To which weaknesses was Brother Lawrence prone?

5. What are the sources from which *The Practice of the Presence of God* is derived?

6. In what ways can you practice the presence of God in your daily life?

7. What are the most important things taught to us by the life and writings of Brother Lawrence?

Part I

Collected Thoughts

1. What was Brother Lawrence's "whole business"?

2. What is the shortest and easiest way to attain to Christian perfection?

3. What, according to Brother Lawrence, is the end of all the thoughts and affections of the soul?

4. What is the sole means through which the Lord is revealed to us?

5. What is the greatest glory we can give to God?

6. What gives us great relief in the trials and sorrows of life?

7. In what ways can you give glory to God?

8. Have you discovered the blessings of walking in the presence of God?

Part II
Beginning of Perfection

1. Of what is the life of Brother Lawrence a pattern?

2. From what did Brother Lawrence's conversion spring?

3. What was the one "light" Brother Lawrence took for his path?

4. What is "the spirit of the Church"?

5. Which books of the Bible were Brother Lawrence's favorites?

6. What can you learn from the life of Brother Lawrence?

7. Is it possible to be perfect?

8. What Bible verses do you know that apply to the presence of God?

Pursuing the Sense of the Presence of God

1. How can the presence of God be reached most readily?

2. What role did faithfulness play in Brother Lawrence's learning to practice the presence of God?

3. How did Brother Lawrence get his imagination under control?

4. How can we give service to God continually?

5. Why is faithfulness so important?

6. Are you pursuing the presence of God?

Forsaking All of Self for God

1. In what way do we discover what we lack and what we need?

2. From what does introspection stem?

3. What did Brother Lawrence have to forget in order to find God?

4. What enabled Brother Lawrence to experience perfect peace?

5. Is it possible to have peace in all circumstances?

6. What distractions prevent you from keeping your mind stayed on God?

Do All for the Love of God

1. What was the proof of Brother Lawrence's noble soul?

2. What was Brother Lawrence's one purpose?

3. What warned Brother Lawrence about the "sunken rocks" of the spiritual life?

4. What is the way to avoid such perils?

5. Have you found your purpose in life?

6. Is your life purpose driven?

Brother Lawrence's Final Days

1. In what specific ways did Brother Lawrence face death?

2. Which Psalm did Brother Lawrence frequently repeat on his death bed?

3. What were the last words of Brother Lawrence?

4. Have you found freedom from the fear of death?

5. How do we defeat the enemy called death?

Part of the Great Band Who Have Forsaken the World for Christ

1. What, according to St. Clement of Alexandria, is the great business of a philosopher?

2. What is the effect in one's life of continual contemplation through prayer?

3. What would Brother Lawrence teaching be to those who are filled with the cares of this world?

4. What obligation is laid on every person?

5. What do you think Brother Lawrence meant by these words: "The all for the all"?

6. According to Brother Lawrence, what should cause us to count a day as lost?

7. Have you forsaken the world for Christ?

Part III—Conversations With Brother Lawrence
First Conversation

1. How old was Brother Lawrence when he was converted?

2. How do we establish ourselves in a sense of God's presence?

3. With what should we feed and nourish our souls?

4. What should be the rule of our conduct?

5. In what should we seek our satisfaction?

6. How does one attain to the resignation required by God?

7. Have you discovered the joy of the Lord?

Second Conversation

1. By what was Brother Lawrence governed?

2. What thought had long troubled Brother Lawrence? How did he overcome this thought?

3. What must we do in order to form a habit of conversing with God continually?

4. What was Brother Lawrence's prayer when an occasion of practicing some virtue was offered?

5. What would Brother Lawrence do and say when he failed in his duty?

6. What role does confession play in your life?

Third Conversation

1. What was the foundation of Brother Lawrence's spiritual life?

2. What draws down great graces in our lives?

3. What did Brother Lawrence think was the worst thing that could ever happen to him?

4. What did Brother Lawrence fear?

5. What is a sure way to Heaven, according to Brother Lawrence?

6. What must be the end purpose of all actions?

7. Why do many not progress in the spiritual life?

8. Are you growing in Christ?

Fourth Conversation

1. On what does our sanctification depend?

2. What was Brother Lawrence's "most excellent method ... of going to God"?

3. What is the whole substance of religion?

4. When a soul aspires after perfection, upon what must it be dependent?

5. What does God expect of us?

Other Accounts of Brother Lawrence

1. What was Brother Lawrence's answer to the man who asked him by what means he had attained to such a habitual sense of the presence of God?

2. What was Brother Lawrence's prayer when he began his work?

3. What did people see when they looked at Brother Lawrence?

4. What do people see when they look at you?

Part IV—Letters of Brother Lawrence
First Letter

1. From what did Brother Lawrence receive continual assistance upon all occasions?

2. How do we hinder God and stop the flow of His grace?

3. How does your life compare with Brother Lawrence's example?

4. What is your source of strength?

Second Letter

1. What are the three stages of life that lead to blessed fulfillment?

2. How did Brother Lawrence begin his religious service?

3. How did Brother Lawrence regard himself?

4. What, according to Brother Lawrence, was "the bosom of God"?

5. Is your life being transformed?

Third Letter

1. What subject, according to Brother Lawrence, contains the whole spiritual life?
2. What must God do with our hearts in order to possess them as His own?
3. In what activity do we find the sweetest and most delightful life?
4. On what subject would Brother Lawrence have preached if he were a preacher?
5. Why is Brother Lawrence's life so fascinating to us?

Fourth Letter

1. What response was intolerable to Brother Lawrence?
2. What "good things" must we lay aside in order to put our whole trust in God?
3. Have you died to yourself?

Fifth Letter

1. What must we continually search for?
2. Through tranquility, what was Brother Lawrence able to avoid?
3. Why are peace, serenity, and tranquility important to us? What are their benefits in our lives?

Sixth Letter

1. What kinds of prayers are acceptable to God?
2. What fortifies a soldier's courage?
3. Do you pray without ceasing?

Seventh Letter

1. What part of our being rules our faculties?
2. What will help to prevent us from having a wandering mind?
3. What should be the continual focus of our minds?
4. How do you keep your mind stayed on God?

Eighth Letter

1. What should be our only business in life?
2. Upon what must we rely in order to escape the dangers that abound in life?
3. What must we do in order to know God?
4. What is the difference between knowing God and knowing about Him?
5. What is the difference between religion and a personal relationship with God?

Ninth Letter

1. When we are with God, what will our experience of suffering be?
2. When we are not with God, what will our experience of pleasure be?
3. How old was Brother Lawrence when he wrote this letter?
4. What kinds of things do we learn from suffering?

Tenth Letter

1. What should be our first love?
2. What is the glorious work of a Christian?
3. Are you walking in love?

Eleventh Letter

1. How does one find sweetness and consolation in suffering?
2. What comforted Brother Lawrence in this life?
3. How does God bring comfort to His children?

Twelfth Letter

1. In what different ways did Brother Lawrence view God?
2. What keeps us from offending the Lord and doing anything to displease Him?
3. What enables us to ask successfully for the graces we need?
4. What is your personal definition of "grace"?

Thirteenth Letter

1. What alleviates bodily diseases?
2. What are the results of suffering?
3. In what ways does God draw us to himself?
4. What is your typical response to suffering?

Fourteenth Letter

1. For what reason does God sometimes permit us to suffer from infirmities?
2. What should we ask God for rather than deliverance from pain?
3. What sweeten s pain?
4. Who is the only physician of all our illnesses?

Fifteenth Letter

1. According to Brother Lawrence, what is paradise?

2. Where is the spiritual temple in which we may adore God incessantly?

3. What does God never refuse to those who ask for it earnestly?

4. Jesus said, "The Kingdom of God is within you." What did He mean by this?

Sixteenth Letter

1. What kind of knowledge would help us to receive equally from God's hand both the sweet and the bitter?

2. How do you practice the presence of God in your life?

3. What should all our occupation be?

4. Where can we find God?

5. Do you experience God's presence daily?

Part V—Ways of Attaining the Presence of God
Essential Conditions for Attaining the Presence of God

1. When we know we have displeased God, what should we do?

2. What is the first condition for attaining to the presence of God?

3. What is the second condition for attaining to the presence of God?

4. What is the most spiritual, most real, most free, and most life-giving manner of prayer?

Necessary Practices for Attaining the Spiritual Life

1. What practice is the most holy, most general, and most needful in the spiritual life?

2. Where should the soul find its joy?

3. What should all of our actions become?

4. What enables us to bruise the head of the evil one?

5. How do we destroy the love of self?

6. What must be our guide?

7. By what should our acts of worship be prompted and guided?

8. Where do we find strength when we are weak?

Always Consider the Glory of God

1. What is the sacrifice that we should be offering to God?

2. What should we do as we enter upon the spiritual life?

3. On what is the soul most dependent as it aspires to perfection?

4. What does grace do in the believer's life?

5. What is your experience of the glory of God?

We Are Required to Worship God in Spirit and in Truth

1. What does the admonition to worship God in spirit and in truth mean?

2. How do we worship God in truth?

3. Do you spend time worshiping God in spirit and in truth?

Union of the Soul With God

1. What are the three degrees involved in the union of the soul with God?

2. What is virtual union?

3. What is actual union?

4. What must we deny in order to be united with God?

The Presence of God

1. What are some other terms for practicing the presence of God?

2. Where does the soul speak to God?

3. What is the life and nourishment of the soul?

Benefits of the Presence of God

1. How does the soul draw near to the state of the Blessed?

2. What is the first benefit of the presence of God?

3. In what does the practice of the presence of God strengthen us?

4. What is the work of hope in our lives?

5. What are five other benefits of the presence of God?

Index

A

acts of faith 72
affliction 97, 108, 119, 133, 134, 160, 165
appetites 75, 145

B

body 17, 64, 75, 76, 93, 108, 127, 145, 169

C

communion 27, 44, 76, 87, 94, 117, 129, 131, 140
communion with God 25, 26, 60, 92, 103, 129, 140
courage 13, 43, 98, 104, 113, 115, 116, 117

D

desires 71, 89, 91, 93, 115

F

Faith 15, 22
faith 14, 15, 16, 17, 23, 24, 25, 26, 34, 35, 38, 42, 54, 57, 60, 63, 69, 71, 82, 86, 87, 108, 113, 114, 117, 120, 121, 127, 131, 140, 141, 143, 1 44, 171
faithfulness 22, 26, 127, 130

N

novice 14, 76

O

obedience 72, 128

P

perfection 13, 15, 22, 23, 28, 29, 35, 43, 54, 67, 70, 101, 131, 134
piety 21, 85
prayer 14, 16, 39, 41, 42, 48, 49, 54, 59, 60, 68, 71, 72, 73, 74, 86, 88, 89, 99, 100, 103, 110, 128, 130, 144, 157, 160

Q

quiet times 130

R

religion 35, 69, 81, 85, 101, 110

S

self 28, 29, 30, 31, 44, 45, 130, 169
self-denial 75, 145
self-love 29, 89
senses 121, 128, 130, 145
sin 13, 30, 60, 74, 102, 109, 129, 135, 172
sinner 30, 110
soul 13, 14, 17, 22, 23, 24, 26, 29, 30, 33, 35, 38, 39, 43, 53, 54, 63, 64, 68, 70, 81, 82, 83, 86, 87, 88, 89, 93, 95, 108, 115, 128, 129, 130, 131, 134, 135, 137, 138, 139, 140, 141, 143, 144, 145, 152, 154, 159, 161, 172

spiritual life 17, 25, 34, 35, 45, 63, 64, 69, 83, 85,
     91, 109, 129, 133
submission 71, 134
Sufferings 104
sufferings 86, 103, 108, 113, 114, 117, 119

T

temptation 42
temptations 70, 129
trouble 27, 37, 57, 69, 86, 140
troubles 45, 70, 86, 103

U

union with God 60

V

virtue 13, 15, 21, 22, 28, 35, 43, 58, 65, 115

W

will of God 30, 69, 134
world 13, 21, 27, 28, 30, 41, 42, 44, 45, 53, 54, 57,
     61, 83, 92, 97, 102, 105, 107, 109, 113, 128,
     134, 140, 168, 169, 170, 172
worship 27, 97, 133, 135, 136, 144

Pure Gold Classics

AN EXPANDING COLLECTION OF THE
BEST-LOVED CHRISTIAN CLASSICS OF ALL TIME.

AVAILABLE AT FINE BOOKSTORES.
FOR MORE INFORMATION, VISIT WWW.BRIDGELOGOS.COM

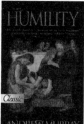
HUMILITY
Classic
ANDREW MURRAY

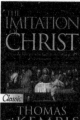
THE
IMITATION
of
CHRIST
Classic
THOMAS
a' KEMPIS

Classic
IN
HIS
STEPS
CHARLES M. SHELDON

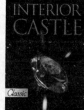
INTERIOR
CASTLE
Classic
TERESA OF AVILA

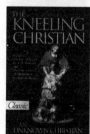
THE
KNEELING
CHRISTIAN
Classic
AN UNKNOWN CHRISTIAN

MADAME
JEANNE
GUYON
Classic

MORNING
BY
MORNING
Classic
CHARLES H.
SPURGEON

THE
OVERCOMING
LIFE
Classic
D.L. MOODY

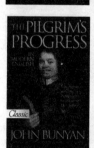
THE PILGRIM'S
PROGRESS
IN MODERN ENGLISH
Classic
JOHN BUNYAN

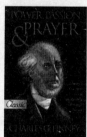
POWER, PASSION
& PRAYER
Classic
CHARLES G. FINNEY

THE
PRACTICE
of the
PRESENCE
of GOD
Classic
BROTHER LAWRENCE

SECRET
POWER
Classic
D.L. MOODY

A SERIOUS CALL
to a
DEVOUT
& HOLY LIFE
Classic
WILLIAM LAW

SINNERS
in the
HANDS *of an*
ANGRY GOD
Classic
JONATHAN
EDWARDS

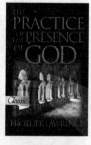
THE
SOVEREIGNTY
of GOD
Classic
A.W. PINK

TABLE
TALK
MARTIN
LUTHER
Classic

TOZER ON THE
HOLY SPIRIT
Classic
A.W. TOZER

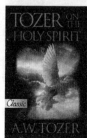
INCLUDES AUDIO EXCERPTS CD
WALKING
WITH GOD
Classic
ANDREW MURRAY

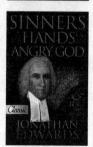
WITH
CHRIST *in the*
SCHOOL *of*
PRAYER
Classic
ANDREW MURRAY

WILLIAM
WILBERFORCE
Classic
GREATEST WORKS

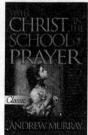

Pure Gold Classics

CHRISTIAN CLASSICS

A classic is a work of enduring excellence; a Christian classic is a work of enduring excellence that is filled with divine wisdom, biblical revelation, and insights that are relevant to living a godly life. Such works are both spiritual and practical. Our Pure Gold Classics contain some of the finest examples of Christian writing that have ever been published, including the works of John Foxe, Charles Spurgeon, D.L. Moody, Martin Luther, John Calvin, Saint John of the Cross, E.M. Bounds, John Wesley, Andrew Murray, Hannah Whitall Smith, and many others.

The timeline on the following pages will help you to understand the context of the times in which these extraordinary books were written and the historical events that must have served to influence these great writers to create works that will always stand the test of time. Inspired by God, many of these authors did their work in difficult times and during periods of history that were not sympathetic to their message. Some even had to endure great persecution, misunderstanding, imprisonment, and martyrdom as a direct result of their writing.

The entries that are printed in green type will give you a good overview of Christian history from the birth of Jesus to modern times.

The entries in red pertain to writers of Christian classics from Saint Augustine, who wrote his *Confessions* and *City of God*, to Charles Sheldon, twentieth-century author of *In His Steps*.

Entries in black provide a clear perspective on the development of secular history from the early days of Buddhism (first century) through the Civil Rights Movement.

Finally, the blue entries highlight secular writers and artists, including Chaucer, Michelangelo, and others.

Our color timeline will provide you with a fresh perspective of history, both secular and Christian, and the classics, both secular and Christian. This perspective will help you to understand each author better and to see the world through his or her eyes.

A Kodansha Comics Trade Paperback Original
To Your Eternity 11 copyright © 2019 Yoshitoki Oima
English translation copyright © 2019 Yoshitoki Oima

Published in the United States by Kodansha Comics, an imprint of Kodansha USA Publishing, LLC, New York.

Publication rights for this English edition arranged through Kodansha Ltd., Tokyo.

First published in Japan in 2019 by Kodansha Ltd., Tokyo as *Fumetsu no Anata e*, volume 11.

ISBN 978-1-63236-798-3

Cover Design: Tadashi Hisamochi (hive&co., Ltd.)
Title Logo Design: Shinobu Ohashi

Printed in the United States of America.

www.kodanshacomics.com

9 8 7 6 5 4 3 2 1
Translation: Steven LeCroy
Lettering: Darren Smith
Editing: Haruko Hashimoto, Alexandra Swanson
Editorial Assistance: YKS Services LLC/SKY Japan, INC.
Kodansha Comics Edition Cover Design: Phil Balsman

KC
KODANSHA
COMICS

Publisher: Kiichiro Sugawara
Managing editor: Maya Rosewood
Vice president of marketing & publicity: Naho Yamada

Director of publishing services: Ben Applegate
Associate director of operations: Stephen Pakula
Publishing services managing editor: Noelle Webster
Assistant production manager: Emi Lotto

Soon, a battle spanning the centuries
will enter a new phase...

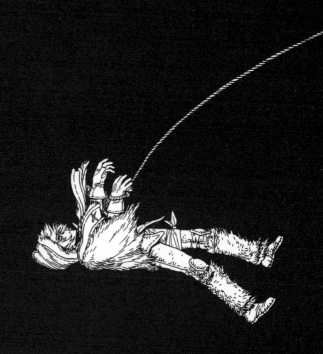

THE RENRIL ARC HEADS TO ITS FINAL STAGE.

A long sought-after reunion
with "Mother"...

...but with an immortal body on
the verge of falling to betrayal.